PRAYER
in
WORLD RELIGIONS

Denise Lardner Carmody
John Tully Carmody

ORBIS BOOKS

Maryknoll, New York 10545

The Catholic Foreign Mission Society of America (Maryknoll) recruits and trains people for overseas missionary service. Through Orbis Books Maryknoll aims to foster the international dialogue that is essential to mission. The books published, however, reflect the opinions of their authors and are not meant to represent the official position of the society.

Library of Congress Cataloging-in-Publication Data

Carmody, Denise Lardner, 1935 –
    Prayer in world religions / Denise Lardner Carmody, John Tully
Carmody.
        p.   cm.
    Includes bibliographical references.
    ISBN 0-88344-644-8
    1. Prayer—Comparative studies.   I. Carmody, John, 1939-
II. Title.
BL560.C27 1990
291.4'3 – dc20   89-48198
                                                                    CIP

For John and Julie Sanford

7

CONTENTS

PREFACE

This book is a brief survey of the nature and function of prayer in the world religions. To keep the contents manageable, we have contented ourselves with treating Judaism, Islam, Hinduism, Buddhism, Native American Religions, and African Religions. We have assumed a Christian audience and so have not treated Christian prayer.

In each chapter we follow the same format. First, we suggest the historical and doctrinal background necessary to understand the tradition's views and practices regarding prayer. Second, we deal with stories (myths) suggesting the concrete ways that the tradition in question has thought about prayer and the concerns that compose prayer. Third, we deal with representative prayers. Fourth, we describe representative rituals, to suggest the ceremonial context for the tradition's more formal or communal prayers. Fifth and last, we offer "Christian reflections," tying the given tradition's experiences with prayer to the experiences of Christians.

Our introductory and concluding chapters provide context and summary reflections. Among the contextual features of our study of prayer is the current interest in interreligious dialogue, which suggests both the horizon in which analyses of prayer ought to take place nowadays and some of the most fruitful foci. Our summary reflections underscore the worldwide imperative to pray and the abounding of grace in humanity's prayer.

Our hope is that this little book will both inform the general reader about the salient features of prayer, East and West, and encourage such a reader to think well of prayer—well enough to make it a personal vocation. We owe thanks to Bob Gormley, Robert Ellsberg, and Eve Drogin of Orbis Books for welcoming this project and shepherding it to publication. We also thank the myriad people, whether known face to face or from books, who have convinced us that prayer should be as basic as eating and sleeping.

Chapter 1

INTRODUCTION

CONTEMPORARY INTERRELIGIOUS DIALOGUE

For the last decade of the twentieth century, dialogue among the world's religions is both a certainty and a necessity. It is a necessity because the impact of religion on world politics has shown that understanding other people's faith is a sine qua non for dealing with them successfully. The turmoil over Salman Rushdie's novel *The Satanic Verses,* which millions of Muslims claimed blasphemed Islam and the prophet Muhammad, illustrates such necessity.

The certainty of dialogue among the world's religions stems from the progress that representatives of the major traditions already have achieved. In scholarly circles, the 1980s saw steady progress in the study of the world religions, much of it accomplished through cross-cultural exchanges, international conferences, publishing ventures that enlisted representatives of several traditions, and the increasing efforts of universities to provide academic courses dealing with the history, culture, and doctrines of the major faiths. Indeed, simply among Christians a steady spate of books appeared that argued for global approaches to faith in Jesus and for the development of a universal theology that would reflect the pluralism of world religion.[1]

Still, much work remains to be done. Not only does dialogue among the world religions have to illumine the political solutions to conflicts that have some roots in faith, but it also has to

1

illumine the common stake that people of different traditions have in one another's religious experience. The political solutions include both bringing religious pressure to bear on issues of social and economic justice and working out ground rules for free speech. Until the religions manifestly are challenging the great gaps between the haves and the have-nots in today's world, their messages about God or ultimate reality easily will be dismissed as merely sounding brass and tinkling cymbal. Until the religions have overcome their tendencies toward dogmatism, intolerance, and the suppression of individual rights, they will not strike mature, sophisticated, internationalized citizens of any tradition as angels of light. To be blunt about it, we believe that many of the world's religions, Christian groups quite included, remain important parts of the problem of international violence and poverty. Equally, many remain sources of intolerance and hatred, rather than sources of mutual respect and love. The interreligious dialogue of the 1990s either will ameliorate this situation or will rightly be dismissed as perhaps interesting but hardly crucial to solving the problems most likely to entice the nations into large-scale war.

The stake that people of the different traditions have in one another's religious experience is nothing less than insight about the most important factor in human existence, the import of divinity. Religious experience embraces human beings' deepest and most significant encounters with reality—their own meaning, the construction of the physical world in which they live, and the order of their societies. East and West, yesterday and today, those who have the best claim to being heard about how human beings ought to live together are people who have gone to the depths of human existence and wrestled with death, disease, sin, and disorder. As well, they have wrestled with intimations of immortality, infusions of health, examples of sainthood, and occasions when groups achieved right order, produced justice and peace. One cannot talk about the experience of profound insight, life-changing illumination, or about the gift of love that transforms people from within, without referring to religious language. "Revelation," "conversion," and "grace" are the terms that such experiences naturally generate. The fact is that the best in us human beings appears as a gift of God, the result of an extraordinary encounter with reality of a transcendent, more than human order. Muslims venerate Muhammad because he received the revelations of Allah expressed in the Qur'an. Christians venerate Jesus because he received the revelations of his Father and accomplished his Father's will to offer the good news (gospel) of salvation to all people. Buddhists revere Gautama because he received the revelations that led to the Four Noble Truths, the digest of the way to enlightenment and liberation.

These three holy men, founders of religious traditions that have nourished billions of human beings, can stand as paradigms of what happens when a person receives, in extraordinary measure, disclosures of how reality finally is structured, what life finally is about, how people ought to live if they are to enjoy peace and joy. Indeed, they can stand as paradigms and touchstones of what human wisdom always has to preach: that we are more than our own, that the love of an Other is our reason to be, that sin and error do not have the final say, that the source of human success is nearer than the pulse at our throats.

If politicians and economists cannot understand such wisdom, so much the worse for them and the nations they claim to be serving. The bottom line in the spiritual life, the life concerned with wisdom and healing, is that disordered teachers cannot remedy the dysfunctions of the individuals or nations they would teach. A variant of this truism is that sick physicians are poor sources of physical, mental, and spiritual health. "Physician, heal thyself!" the charge has always been. Preacher, church, mosque: get your own house in order! You have to know, from first-hand experience and struggle, what you are talking about, if you are to pontificate about right order, if you are to prescribe how to heal the wounds in human nature that keep so many millions locked in suffering.

The stake that ordinary people have in the dialogue among the world religions that has grown in recent years therefore is enormous. One always risks exaggerating the importance of the particular drum that fate has given one to beat, but readers who agree that death, evil, and disorder set human beings their primary tasks should easily see that clarifying the traditions that have spoken most insightfully about such phenomena is a work of the highest priority. How to communicate the findings of dialogue about such matters to the politicians and business leaders responsible for large portions of world affairs is a further question, worthy of many further books. First, though, the participants in the dialogue about the resources humanity has developed for living justly and beautifully have to gain some consensus about what the politicians and business leaders ought to hear. First, those commissioned by talent and providence to explore the issuance of right order from direct contact with the divine powers responsible for both the world's origin and its healing have to put aside their provincialism and open their souls sufficiently to hear the words God has been speaking to their sisters and brothers of other traditions, that they may realize how similar those words are to the revelations on which their own tradition depends.

Ironically, then, the dialogue developing among representatives of the world religions demands that all the participants themselves become learned in the things for humanity's sanctification and peace. Unless the participants, academic or lay, move beyond superficial exchanges of information and develop some accord about the heart of the human matter, they might as well print up their proceedings and head back to their ordinary preoccupations. Those hungry for words of instruction about the heart of the human matter, the meaning of life and death, will continue to languish for lack of nourishment. They have minds wanting to know what keeps the world in existence and might give its evolution an overarching meaning. They have hearts wanting to feel a love that promises to defeat death and prove stronger than evil. The saints of the great religious traditions speak of such things, demonstrate such forces. Those participating in the dialogue of the saints' traditions ought to spend more time reflecting on how divinity or ultimate reality can transform scarred human nature than on minutiae of history and doctrine.

PRAYER EAST AND WEST

The action manifesting a transformed human nature is aimed at, and successfully contributes to, peace and justice. Peace and justice, we might say, are the outer expressions, the body, of the grace and order divinity grants to the saints. In this book, we assume the significance of peace and justice, in part because in another work we have discussed what the scriptures of the non-Christian religions have to say about peace and justice.[2] Our focus here is the means and substance of inner order: formation, integration, by God or ultimate reality. By consensus, the place to look for such formation in the world religions is in their prayer or meditation. (As a first distinction, consider "prayer" to be address of a personal deity and "meditation" outreach toward an impersonal ultimate reality.) What Muslims, Christians, and Jews do in their public worship and private searches for God best focuses the area, the psychic and ontological zones, where encounters with God can transform such people into sources of justice and peace. What Hindus and Buddhists do in their rituals and yogic meditations best focuses the area where encounters with ultimate reality, the mysterious source of the world and enlightenment, can transform Hindus and Buddhists into sources of justice and peace. Analogously, the prayers of Africans and Native Americans instruct us in where they have sought the order, repair, and nourishment that most helped them treat one another fairly, most enabled them to live together helpfully and tranquilly.

We are not saying that prayer is the whole of any religious tradition. We are not denying that God can raise up children of Abraham from inert stones, if God wishes. We are simply saying that the leading shamans, prophets, and sages of the world religions have all been people of singular interiority. If asked what held their souls and lives together, they would respond in harmony: meeting the divine, consorting with the holy mystery at the foundations of the world and self. Thus the shamans who danced and sang themselves into trance did so not simply to function as healers, reconcilers, guides of the spirits of the dead to the land of rest, but, more personally, because what they experienced in trance, the ecstasies it brought, quickened their spirits and gave them joy. Not to dance and sing was to grow sad, feel torpor, experience the *Zerissenheit*, the torn-to-pieces-hood, of desolation. Shamanizing has put shamans back together. Meditation has put monks back together. Prayer the world over has functioned as the poor person's psychoanalysis, much cheaper and better warranted than sessions on a Freudian couch.

Does this mean we are considering prayer mainly as therapy (and scoffing at contemporary psychiatry)? Not at all. Prayer primarily is the praise and adoration of God, while contemporary psychiatry deserves all the respect one gives any decent healing profession. But the reality has been that people who prayed have reported that their prayer put them back together. East and West, the witness is that human nature needs a grace of healing, as well as a grace that elevates it so that it can commune with divinity. In Christian tradition, healing grace (*gratia sanans*) and elevating grace (*gratia elevans*) are both attributed to the Spirit of Christ. When one meets the Christian God (the Spirit as God both given and received), the free encounter restores perspective and balance from within. As well, it takes one's thirst for transcendence, for moving out of mortality, ignorance, and sin, and raises it to a higher (a "supernatural") plane. For Christian conviction, the Spirit comes to our spirits for gracious exchanges of light, and love communicates divine life itself. What occurs is nothing less than drawing human beings into the perfect fullness of the divine light and love. This process, known in Eastern Christianity as *theosis* (divinization), heals human nature by making it more than human. By a logic hidden in the mystery of the Incarnation, God reveals that the destiny of human nature, the fulfillment it spontaneously seeks (by always pressing to know and love more), is to become a sharer of the divine nature (see I Peter 2:4). What happened when the Logos took flesh of the Virgin Mary and became fully human dramatizes what all human beings want and may be granted. The Johannine literature of the New Testament makes it quite plain: those who abide in the Spirit of Christ enjoy relations with the Father, Son, and Spirit — relations that inevitably entail sharing in the divine deathlessness.

Two further comments will complete our Introduction. The first is that the Christian theology of grace (both healing and elevating) considers the Spirit of Christ to be operating outside the borders of formal Christianity, wherever people open their hearts to the manifest mystery of their existence and gamble their lives on honesty and love. The second is that whereas one may encounter the transforming Spirit of God in any decent occupation, the testimony of all the religious traditions is that prayer (petition, meditation, contemplation, ritual, attentive silence — the forms are numerous) is the occupation most directly opening the person to the transforming Spirit. Consequently, prayer is the crux of the spiritual life, whenever the spiritual life is conceived as intending humanity's deepest illumination and healing.

Let us elaborate on these two comments. First, the Christian view that grace is universal stems from the earliest Christian appreciations of the significance of Christ. In saying that Christ died once and for all human beings, the early Christians certainly were amazingly bold. Their justification for such boldness was experiential: the resurrected Christ had told the disciples to preach to all nations; the Spirit poured out by the risen Christ had fallen on people of all nations; Peter had experienced that God does not play favorites but may give the Spirit to any people that call upon the divine name; the teachings and healings of Jesus had a universal import that escaped the Jewish categories in which both Jesus himself and the first disciples inevitably cast them. When Paul spoke of Christ as the New Adam, centering a new economy in which sin had abounded and grace now abounded the more, he made the death and resurrection of Jesus of Nazareth the axis of all of history. If Adam symbolized the solidarity of the human race in a history of struggle and self-division, Christ symbolized the possibility of a future history of hope and triumph. By moving the mystery of salvation outside strictly Jewish categories, the early Christians developed universalist tendencies from within Judaism itself so that the implications for the Gentiles became plain. No longer would the distinction between Jews and Gentiles connote a substantial difference in the operations of grace in people's lives. Henceforth, the Spirit focused by Jesus Christ could be believed to work in all people's hearts, luring them toward the divine beauty and holiness. No rightful respect for the legitimacy and estimable achievements of Judaism after the rise of Christianity ought to muffle the outreach of grace that Pauline Christianity implied.[3] In the wake of such an outreach, both Christians and Jews ought to be humbler about their role in the mystery of salvation, the work of healing and elevation.

Second, concerning the centrality of prayer to the work of healing and elevation, we may note how important prayer was in the lives of the founders of the great world religions. For example, Muhammad only received the revelations constituting the Qur'an after he had taken himself out into the countryside to pray. Moses was always interceding for his people, throughout their trek in the wilderness, following up on God's invitation to speak with divinity face to face, like a friend, and extending his arms in petition. Jesus regularly drew aside to pray, and his disciples finally realized that all his actions were shaped by the Spirit anointing him. The Buddha only came to enlightenment after he had seated himself under the bo tree and resolved not to leave until he had solved the problem of suffering. The typical Hindu *sadhu* (saint), who extends the tradition of the seers credited with creating the Vedas, is a profound yogi in search of interior peace and liberation. At the foundations of the world religions, then, stands eloquent testimony to the impact of silent, solitary, passionate pursuit of the divine mystery. We want to ponder such foundations, under the intuition that they continue to offer humanity the best sources for justice and peace. If the love that divinity seems to communicate, when people do persevere in prayer, is the most profound and crucial force in creation—the best explanation for both creativity and healing—then our study of prayer in the world religions should take us to the very heart of the human matter.

Beginnings of prayer

Chapter 2

JUDAISM

BACKGROUND

Judaism traces its origins to the covenant made with Abraham and recorded in the book of Genesis. Much in that record is mythological (interested in a different truth than what scientific history seeks), but Jews have always located their sense of chosenness in the relationship that God established with Abraham. Abraham was a monotheist—a person convinced that divinity had to be one. From its roots in the experiences that Abraham represents, Judaism has made the first article of its confession of faith the Oneness of its Lord.

It was under Moses, however, that Jewish peoplehood fully came into being. The Exodus from Egypt and establishment of the Mosaic covenant on Mount Sinai have stood in Jewish memory as the equivalent of the American Revolution and Constitutional Congress. Whatever the actual historical events composing the departure from bondage in Egypt, Jews have used the Exodus as the great paradigm by which they ought to configure their experiences down through the centuries. Certainly there were other paradigms, including the kingdom that the Lord established through David, but the main axis of traditional Jewish interpretation has run through the Exodus and granting of the Covenant (with its Torah— its instruction or Law).

The covenants that God established with Abraham and Moses included promises that a distinct people would come to possess its own land. The Bible records the possession of this promised land under the leadership of Joshua, and then the fortunes of succeeding generations in the land. The "judges" (charismatic leaders) who guided Israel (the descendants of Jacob, the grandson of Abraham) after the conquest of the promised land depended on God's promises to Moses. The kingdom that briefly flourished under David and Solomon seemed a brilliant fulfillment of the hopes that had grown through the centuries, but then the kingdom split apart, kingship turned corrupt, and eventually foreign enemies came to rule both the northern and the southern portions of what had been David's unified realm.

The prophetic and priestly writers reponsible for the biblical record of Israel's wavering fortunes were remarkable in pondering straightforwardly the inability of their people to live up to the obligations and potential of the covenant begun with Abraham and fully articulated under Moses. Self-criticism attends the entire record of Israel's history, down to the nadir of the exile to Babylon in the sixth century B.C.E. (Before the Common Era). The refrain of the historians tracing the fate of the kingdom divided after Solomon is that the people sinned in the sight of the Lord. The primeval history recorded in the early chapters of Genesis places such sin back to the foundations of the human race. The great writing prophets (Isaiah, Jeremiah, Ezekiel) are obsessed with the problem of why the covenant, so rich in promise, was so regularly underachieved. Overall, the Law and the Prophets (the first two portions of the Hebrew Bible) are an amazingly rich resource for understanding the light that relationship with a holy God sheds on human nature. The Bible seldom blinks: God is much better than human beings are able to appreciate or sustain.

The Writings (the third portion of the Hebrew Bible) reflect the sobriety inculcated by Israel's experience of foreign rule. Assyria, Babylon, Persia, Greece, and Rome all held hegemony over Israel, making the notion of a promised land painful and paradoxical. By the time the Romans finally crushed Jewish resistance to their rule, in the second century C.E. (Common Era), the biblical era was long gone. The teachers (rabbis) who had filled the vacuum left by the destruction of the Temple in Jerusalem and the sacrificial worship upon which it centered pointed to the Torah as the backbone of Jewish identity. Commentary on the Torah had become the mainstay of religious intellectualism, and in the diaspora (exile outside of Jerusalem and Judea) this commentary richly grew. The compilation of many centuries' work in the Talmud (complete around 500 C.E.) gave subsequent generations of Jews a book nearly equal to the Bible in significance. The Talmud gathered the oral teaching long considered complementary to the Torah recorded in the Bible (Tanakh—the Law, Prophets, and Writings). Jews scattered across many different lands, speaking many different local languages, but clung to a common heritage: Tanakh and Talmud. For the vast majority, keeping the laws spawned by a sense of covenant with the holy Lord was the main way to maintain Jewish identity. Not until modernity (the impact of the eighteenth century Enlightenment) did Jews significantly question the centrality or adequacy of their Torah. As they kept the Sabbath, ate kosher food, separated themselves from the Gentiles, and celebrated their traditional holidays, their Torah structured every aspect of their lives.

For example, when Jewish men prayed three times a day, they were fulfilling an expectation at the heart of the Torah. One prayed to the Lord out of a long memory of all that the Lord had done for his (the Jewish God was strongly patriarchal) people. The Exodus was the most brilliant episode in the history that Jews recalled, but those at prayer also could call to mind creation itself, the original blessing of God upon the world. The Psalms that Jewish memory associated with David and the worship in the Temple in Jerusalem provided a full range of emotions considered suitable for prayer. Perhaps most important were the outbreak of the spirit in praise of God and the spirit's cries of distress. All creation ought to praise the Lord, for his goodness in creating it, for his beauty and majesty, for his faithful kindness and steadfast love toward Israel, his chosen people, for the regularity of the stars and the seasons. When either individuals or the community as a whole came into hard times, the Lord was the first object of recourse. Traditional Jews hoped that the deliverance God had worked in the Exodus, in bringing the people back from the Exile, and at many other times in past history might occur in their own time, to save them from the enemies and threats darkening their own spirits.

Whether using the Psalms or drawing upon other resources, biblical or talmudic, traditional Jews prayed with a sense that they constituted a unique community. In part because of their uniqueness, they had suffered as much in the Common Era as in biblical times. Under both Christians and Muslims, they were always in danger of persecution, never knowing when some new wave of hatred would break out. All of the splendid culture — the literature, mysticism, art, music, philosophy, and science — developed by Jews in the Common Era was tinged by such a possibility. Virtually nowhere did Jews enjoy security and autonomy in the measure possible to Gentiles. After the Enlightenment some Jews hoped that a new egalitarianism and pluralism would prevail in the West, but even when civil laws changed, antisemitic discrimination continued. Matters were especially bad in Eastern Europe, where a great portion of the Jewish population resided. In the minds of many Jewish interpreters of the Nazi holocaust, the "Final Solution" (*Endlösung*) sought by Hitler was simply the culmination of centuries of European hatred.

From the nineteenth century Jews began to divide on the question of how to relate their tradition to modernity. What has come to be known as Orthodox Judaism is the self-conscious effort to maintain the talmudic traditions, somewhat in opposition to the changes urged by the Reform, Conservative, and Reconstructionist movements. Many Orthodox Jews also continue customs of the Hasidim (the "pious ones") who flourished in Eastern Europe from the eighteenth century, inspired by the shining example of the Baal Shem Tov, Hasidism's most charismatic figure. The Hasidim have stressed the joy of living covenanted to the Lord, in reception of the Torah, in a world filled with divine energies laboring for the redemption of all creatures. Their prayer is full of sways and often breaks out in dancing, to let the whole body participate in the praise that the goodness of the Lord warrants.

Nowadays, the modern state of Israel and the United States are the two most important sources of reflection on Jewish existence. The drive of some Soviet Jews for the right to emigrate to Israel gets many headlines, but numerous Soviet Jews have no desire to emigrate, and the problems that the local Arab population presents in Israel seem more critical to the future not only of the state of Israel but also to Jewish self-conception. Right-wing and left-wing Jews divide in their interpretation of how Israel ought to treat embittered Palestinians. Some Jews recur to militant strains of the Bible and argue that it is legitimate, even required, to defend the promised land by harsh force. Other Jews fear that such harshness risks Judaism's soul, making it no more admirable, no more ethical, than its Gentile neighbors.

Ethics, in fact, seems to be something that both religious and secular Jews can agree is of paramount importance. Even contemporary Jews who do not pray or attend religious services tend to have a strong concern for social justice, as though the legacy of the biblical prophets had entered the Jewish genes. The desire of Orthodox Jews in Israel to dominate the religious side of relations with the Israeli government has further complicated the question of what faith, tradition, and prayer ought to mean in a contemporary Jewish state. Disputes about observing the Sabbath, marrying non-Orthodox Jews or Gentiles, and the like have become part of the vexed equations the government struggles to balance. So the question of religious observance, which prayer can dramatically focus, is nothing academic. For present-day Jews, as for their forebears through the centuries, to don the garb for prayer can be a political act.

STORIES

Both biblical stories and stories from later Jewish tradition have supported the conviction that Jews ought to pour out their souls to God in prayer, not shrinking even from arguing with God. For example, there is the story of Abraham's haggling with God over the terms for condemning the wicked city of Sodom: "Then Abraham drew near [to the Lord], and said, 'Wilt thou indeed destroy the righteous with the wicked? Suppose there are fifty righteous within the city; wilt thou then destroy the place and not spare it for the fifty righteous who are in it? Far be it from thee to do such a thing, to slay the righteous with the wicked, so that the righteous fare as the wicked. Far be it from thee! Shall not the Judge of all the earth do right?' And the Lord said, 'If I find at Sodom fifty righteous in the city, I will spare the whole place for their sake.' Abraham answered, 'Behold, I have taken it upon myself to speak to the Lord, I who am but dust and ashes. Suppose five of the fifty righteous are lacking? Wilt thou destroy the whole city for lack of five?' And he said, 'I will not destroy it if I find forty-five there' " (Gen. 18:23–28). The exchange goes on, back and forth, Abraham moving the Lord down the numbers: forty, thirty, twenty, and finally ten. Sodom proves unable to produce even ten righteous, so destruction comes upon it, but Abraham has done his best. Along the way, he has given dozens of generations of Bible readers a dramatic lesson in the familiarity and feistiness the Lord apparently will tolerate. In the wake of Abraham, Jewish prayer legitimately could badger God, all the while that pious people had to declare themselves but dust and ashes.

Moses, Job, and no doubt numerous other biblical figures further exemplify the intimacy and courage that Israelites could show toward their Lord. Moses does not hesitate to complain to God that the burden of leading so stubborn a people through the wilderness has frayed his nerves. Job does not hesitate to accuse God of injustice, and even though God's reply, out of the whirlwind, stresses that human beings are but dust and ashes, God finally approves Job's persistence in demanding justice. The prophet Jeremiah bemoans his vocation, arguing with the Lord that its burdens are too much for him, that (like Moses) he does not have the articulateness the work requires. God provides.

The prophet Elijah had preceded Jeremiah in complaining about the drawbacks of being the bearer of "the word of the Lord," and the response that Elijah received from the Lord became a classical source of the idea that God deals with the religious spirit gently. Elijah has been fleeing from Jezebel, the wicked queen who seeks his life (because he demands fidelity to the Lord and opposes her pagan gods). He is weary, lays himself down to die, and receives a marvelous visitation of an angel, who strengthens him so that he can walk forty days and nights to Mount Horeb (symbolically repeating the Mosaic trek in the wilderness). But whereas the God who dealt with Moses tended to show himself in thunder and lightning, Elijah experiences wonders of a different order: "And he [the Lord] said, 'Go forth, and stand upon the mount before the Lord.' And behold, the Lord passed by, and a great and strong wind rent the mountains, and broke in pieces the rocks before the Lord, but the Lord was not in the wind; and after the wind an earthquake, but the Lord was not in the earthquake; and after the earthquake a fire, but the Lord was not in the fire; and after the fire a still small voice. And when Elijah heard it, he wrapped his face in his mantle and went out and stood at the entrance of the cave. And behold, there came a voice to him, and said, 'What are you doing here, Elijah?' " (I Kings 19: 11–13). Elijah replies that he has been jealous for the Lord, and the Lord implicitly thanks him by sending him back to work with assurances that he will do well. At the least, then, the story of Elijah (who became the very emblem of prophecy) reminded Jews that God could come in many different garbs, stillness prominent among them, and that those serving the Lord could expect spiritual sustenance.

We shall turn to Psalms in the next section, so here let us deal with only one further biblical story. For Jewish mysticism few images were more important than that of the chariot-throne glimpsed by the prophet Ezekiel. The wild symbolism of Ezekiel's vision came to summarize the mysteries of the Godhead itself, in all its holiness, attendance by angelic hosts, and allure for the human spirit. The opening verses of the vision intimate its flavor: "As I looked, behold, a stormy wind came out of the north, and a great cloud, with brightness round about it, and fire flashing forth continually, and in the midst of the fire, as it were gleaming bronze. And from the midst of it came the likeness of four living creatures. And this was their appearance: they had the form of men, but each had four faces, and each of them had four wings ... and above the firmament over their heads there was the likeness of a throne, in appearance like sapphire; and seated above the likeness of a throne was a likeness as it were of a human form. And upward from what had the appearance of his loins I saw as it were gleaming bronze, like the appearance of fire enclosed round about; and downward from what had the appearance of his loins I saw as it were the appearance of fire, and there was brightness round about him. Like the appearance of the bow that is in the cloud on the day of rain, so was the appearance of the brightness round about. Such was the appearance of the glory of the Lord" (Ezek. 1:4–4, 26–28). For many pious Jews, including those devoted to the Cabala (a Jewish esoteric system), the desire of prayer to see the Lord was best fulfilled through Ezekiel's imagery.

When one turns to talmudic views of prayer, one finds stories urging a reverent attitude. For example, "It happened that a pious man was saying his prayers by the roadside. A nobleman passed and greeted him, but he did not respond. The nobleman waited until he had concluded his devotions; and after he had concluded them, he said to him, 'Good-for-nothing! When I greeted you, why did you not return my salutation? If I had cut your head off with a sword, who would have demanded your blood at my hands?' He replied, 'Wait until I have conciliated you with words.' And he continued, 'If you had been standing before a human king, and your friend had greeted you, would you have responded to him?' 'No,' he replied. 'And if you had responded to him, what would they had done to you?' He answered, 'They would have cut off my head with a sword.' He said to him, 'May we not use the argument from the small to the great: If you, standing before a human king, who is here to-day and gone to-morrow in the grave, act thus, how much more so I who was standing before the supreme King of Kings, the Holy One, blessed be He, Who lives and endures for all eternity?' The nobleman was at once appeased, and the pious man departed for his home in peace."[1]

The Hasidim, who made joyous prayer a mainstay of their movement, generally thought of themselves as enlivening the religion inculcated by the Talmud. Where the Talmud stressed legal obligations (*Halakhah*), they tended to stress emotional fervor. Much of this character of Hasidism derived from the personality of the Baal Shem Tov himself. Indeed, the story of his life suggests that in solitude he found an absorbing communion with God: "What seems undeniable about the Baal Shem Tov is that he was a powerful charismatic personality who was orphaned at an early age and so escaped in large measure the fate of being compelled by his parents to adopt the conventional scheme of Jewish learning, which might have stifled his originality. It would seem that the Baal Shem Tov did, in fact, manage to acquire more than the rudiments of a Talmudic education. That he was an outstanding Talmudist is only maintained by uncritical admirers whose chief argument, that he must have been a great scholar in order to attract scholarly disciples, displays a complete lack of understanding of religious psychology. It is said, with justice, of the Baal Shem Tov, that in the Carpathian mountains, where he lived in seclusion, he learned to reflect on the beauties of the creation and that his mystical bent was nourished there in private meditation far from the haunts of men. He was one of those who did see every common bush afire with God and he took off his shoes."[2]

why pray

A subtext of this quotation is the tension that rabbinic Judaism often suffered—a potential antagonism between study and prayer. Ideally study and prayer would go together, but the drive of scholarly rabbis to master the talmudic texts gave rise to the view that studying itself was the prime religious act, more significant than prayer (or, that study was itself an impressive kind of prayer). On the whole, this view served the interests of those put off by Hasidic fervor and more interested in learning and ethics than mysticism.

When Jews from Eastern Europe suffered the horrors of the Nazi death camps, they tried to cope as we might imagine any human group trying. On occasion, however, one of their number would break out in distinctively Jewish prayer. Thus the following story from a survivor of Treblinka:

why pray: to cope

"It was at the end of November 1942. They chased us away from our work and back to our barracks. Suddenly, from the part of the camp called the death camp, flames shot up. Very high. In a flash, the whole countryside, the whole camp, seemed ablaze. It was already dark. We went into our barracks and ate. And from the window, we kept watching the fantastic backdrop of flames of every imaginable color: red, yellow, green, purple. And suddenly one of us stood up. We knew he'd been an opera singer in Warsaw. His name was Salve, and facing the curtain of fire, he began chanting a song I didn't know: 'My God, my

God, why hast Thou forsaken us? We have been thrust into the fire before, but we have never denied Thy Holy Law.' He sang in Yiddish, while behind him blazed the pyres on which they had begun then, in November 1942, to burn the bodies in Treblinka. That was the first time it happened. We knew that night that the dead would no longer be buried, they'd be burned."[3]

PRAYERS

When it came to actual prayers, Jewish tradition frequently thought of the Psalms. Indeed, the song that the survivor of Treblinka did not recognize began by quoting Psalm 22: "My God, my God, why hast thou forsaken me?" On the cross, Jesus quoted the same psalm, suggesting that for nearly two thousand years Jews instinctively used phrases from the Psalms to carry their sufferings or joys to God.

One studying the Psalms is hard-pressed to decide whether suffering predominates over joy. Though many of the Psalms are laments, many also are songs of pure praise in which the Psalmist, and those using the psalm, seem unable to contain their joy at the holiness or goodness of the Lord. Psalm 150, with which the Psalter concludes, is a good example of pure psalmic praise: "Praise the Lord! Praise God in his sanctuary; praise him in his mighty firmament! Praise him for his mighty deeds; praise him according to his exceeding greatness! Praise him with trumpet sound; praise him with lute and harp! Praise him with timbrel and dance; praise him with strings and pipe! Praise him with sounding cymbals; praise him with loud clashing cymbals! Let everything that breathes praise the Lord! Praise the Lord!"

By the sixth century C.E. the rabbis had established the order of daily prayers in the synagogue and prescribed the saying of the *kaddish*. This prayer is a doxology, a praise of God for the divine holiness. It has taken several different forms throughout Jewish history, including a special form for mourning the dead. The complete text, on which changes or substitutions might be worked to adapt the prayer to special occasions, had a part for the presiding rabbi and a responding part for the congregation:

"Glorified and sanctified be God's great name throughout the world which He has created according to His will. May He establish his kingdom in your lifetime and during your days, and within the life of the entire house of Israel, speedily and soon, and say, Amen."

To this the congregation would respond:

"May His great name be blessed forever and to all eternity. Blessed and praised, glorified and exalted, extolled and honored, adored and lauded be the name of the Holy One, blessed be He, beyond all the blessings and hymns, praises and consolations that are even spoken in the world; and say Amen. May the prayers and supplications of the whole house of Israel be accepted by their Father in heaven; and say, Amen. May there be abundant peace from heaven and life, for us and for all Israel; and say, Amen. He who creates peace in His high places, may He create peace for us and for all Israel; and say Amen."[4]

The rabbis were concerned about their people's prayer, since many of them thought that prayer was the act most befitting the divine majesty. Some of the rabbis' prayers were lovely, touched by the warmth of the affection they felt God had showered upon Israel. For example, the following prayer was meant to introduce the Sabbath: "From Thy Love, O Lord our God, wherewith Thou didst love Thy people Israel, and from the compassion, O our King, which Thou didst feel for the children of Thy covenant, Thou didst give us, O Lord our God, this great and holy seventh day in love."[5]

The rabbinic ideal was that all acts rise to God as done for the sake of heaven, as *mitzvah,* fulfillment of God's covenantal law. This ideal led to many prayers of benediction, and to the notion that much prayer ought precisely to be benediction (blessing: *berakhah*). Thus the Talmud taught: "Over fruit growing on trees one says [before eating them]: 'Blessed are You, God our Lord, King of the Universe, He who creates the fruit of the tree.' ... Over wine one says: 'Blessed are You, who creates the fruit of the vine.' "[6] The same format and intention could extend to any other gifts of God, which were to be seen as expressions of the divine Kingship and care: bread, meals, even storms, earthquakes, hills, and deserts. Since everything had come from God, anything could provide the occasion for blessing God.

Jewish liturgy naturally varied prayer according to the season, the holy day being commemorated, or the special occasion (wedding, bar mitzvah, funeral). Thus in the New Union Prayerbook one finds the following prayer for a Sabbath of repentance:

"Holy and awesome God, we stand in Your presence filled with regret for our many sins and failings. Though there is greatness in us, and a deep longing for goodness, we have often denied our better selves and refused to hear Your voice within us calling us to rise to the full height of our humanity. For there is weakness in us, as well as strength. At times we choose to walk in darkness, our vision obscured. We do not care to look within, and we are unwilling to look beyond at those who need our help. O God, we are too weak to walk unaided. Be with us as a strong and wise Friend, and teach us to walk by the light of Your truth. Lord our God and God of all generations, help us to break the hold that the impulse to do evil has upon our hearts. For You have created us able to do Your will. But in our nature there is a wayward spirit that hinders us and keeps us from doing what we should. O Lord our God, help us to subdue it, so that we may, with a whole heart, make Your will our own."[7]

Although Judaism has tended to think of prayer as something done in community, with the group predominating over the individual and the prayer ascending to God as a blessing from the whole community or a petition for the whole community, it has not neglected the individual. Not only did the rabbis, perhaps especially the Hasidim, exemplify passionate personal prayer and communion with God, but the Jewish writers too produced devotional manuals for the pious laity. In the tradition of such manuals stands the fascinating *Jewish Catalog,* a latter-day effort to provide Jews with updated motivations, rituals, and activities designed to encourage their closer identification with Judaism. On the question of private meditation and devotions calculated to make prayer personally meaningful, the *Catalog* offers such advice as the following:

"Now, at this point you might step into the even higher motive of being sorry for what you have done to Him: how you abused his presence and *life* in you, in order to do the very opposite of His plan of love for you; how you took His very head and heart and soiled them foolishly. How you are more pained for what you did to your Beloved than for the reversal of your own progress. Read any of these Psalms—6, 25, 51, 73, or 130—*a few times*. Then renew your covenant with Him and prepare for bed.

"When you are all ready for sleep, lift your soul in your hands, as it were, and give it to Him, saying, 'In Thy hand do I hide my soul—for the night. Thou hast—doest, and wilt redeem me. YHVH, God of truth.' Visualize your tensions walking out of you, one by one, beginning from your toes—become all limp—out from between your eyes. At last—repeating the verse and asking Him to wake you refreshed at—o'clock, and to take over your breathing and rest, feeling at the same time caressed by His hand—visualize your mattress as His arms.

"On other nights, after the short examination, screen yourself off from sounds and cares by visualizing an angel—a spiritual force field—of grace at your *right,* this force field being impregnable by care and worry; at your *left,* an angel of power and strength; *before you,* an angel of soft light and luminousness; and *behind you,* an angel of healing. Over your head, picture the very presence of the living God. As you visualize this, you say: In the name of YHVH, the God of Israel: At my right hand Michael, at my left Gabriel, ahead of me Ariel, behind me Raphael, above my head the Shekhinah [glory] of God!"[8]

Clearly, the forms and moods of Jewish prayer are rich and varied, offering a full fare. If the prayers of the talmudic rabbis can seem stilted, the meditations of recent catalogue writers can seem tinged with yogic techniques. Throughout, though, unifying the whole, is the appreciation of the uniqueness and holiness of the Lord. From him comes the identity that makes Israel Israel. To him ought to go not only benediction, for his many benefits, but also petition, for all the neediness of the world. The Lord could not be the Lord—really, with the impact that confessing his name ought to bring—unless he dominated all of Jewish consciousness. The purpose of Jewish prayer, no less than of Jewish legal observance, was to make a response to the Lord befitting his holiness. If the law sought to make a holy people, who comported themselves as befit the covenant the Lord had given them, Jewish prayer sought to give a fully honest, joyous recompense from the heart. Gradually Judaism developed a doctrine of afterlife, which implied that the covenant went on not only through the physical generations but for individuals after their deaths. Most of Jewish prayer has focused on hallowing the everyday, the here-and-now, however, producing a remarkable love of life and gratitude for life's good things. Children, art, material blessings—all have reflected a glint of God's goodness and so have occasioned prayer and thanksgiving.

RITUALS

We may think of rituals as actions that embody the stories and prayers by which a people constructs its world. Usually religious rituals employ sensate materials, designed to draw the whole worshiper, body and spirit, into their action. For example, the cry of Psalm 150 to praise God with crashing cymbals could justify vibrant Jewish music. The dignity accorded the scrolls of Torah could justify marching with them held high, or even dancing with them. Somewhat special to Jewish worship, however, was the proscription against representations of the divine. With Islam, Judaism has held that the Oneness of the Lord, and the distance of divinity from everything human, makes unseemly paintings, ikons, mosaics, and other ways of visualizing divine things. Archeological excavations have revealed that Judaism did not always interpret this prohibition on images strictly, yet on the whole the gravity of the tradition has been against giving the eye materials for imagining God.

The Sabbath, celebrated as the high point of each week, brought ritual into the Jewish home. When the mother of the house lit the Sabbath candles, covered her eyes, and prayed, the whole family passed from workaday time into sacred time. For twenty-four hours, from sunset on Friday to sunset on Saturday, people were to rest, as the Lord had rested after the six days of creation. Whether the custom of observing the Sabbath predated the materials on creation now found in Genesis can be debated. It is clear, however, that Jews soon thought of their Sabbath as imitating something characteristic of God. As in heaven, so on earth: work was to stop and attention shift to things of higher moment—worship of God, enjoyment of God's blessings, nourishment for the soul. Observant families would attend synagogue, consider the Sabbath meal special, go out of their way to show hospitality to strangers or wayfarers. Studying Torah, spending time with the children, and making love all seemed fitting ways of entering into the Sabbath joy. For in Jewish imagination the Sabbath became God's bride, bedecked in beauty, visiting God's people to console them for their sufferings and raise their sights to their many warrants for joy. God loved them, had bound himself to them with special ties, considered them his own portion. The Sabbath was the Wisdom of God come to help Jews feel these blessings deep in their bones.

In the biblical period Jews developed numerous ritual sacrifices, as ways to render their gratitude to God or petition the Lord's forgiveness. Those who had sinned or become unclean (ritually impure) could use sacrifice as a way of restoring their relationship with the Holy One, blessed be He. The Talmud glossed Malachi 1:11, which speaks of incense offered to the Lord in every place, interpreting the study of Torah as a sacrifice pleasing to the Lord.[9]

Whereas for biblical Israel the feasts of Passover, Shavuot (harvest), and Sukkot (ingathering) occasioned the most important ritual observances, in modern times the observance of New Year (Rosh Hashanah) and the Day of Atonement (Yom Kippur) may be more important. The Passover (Pesach) commemorates the Exodus, the event in which the Lord rescued Israel from bondage and set it on the path toward the reception of the Mosaic covenant, the Torah, and the promised land. The key biblical text is Exodus 12, which establishes that Israel is to memorialize its liberation: "They shall eat the flesh [of the lamb] that night, roasted; with unleavened bread and bitter herbs they shall eat it. Do not eat any of it raw or boiled with water, but roasted, its head with its legs and its inner parts. And you shall let none of it remain until the morning, anything that remains until the morning you shall burn. In this manner you shall eat it: your loins girded, your sandals on your feet, and your staff in your hand; and you shall eat it in haste. It is the Lord's passover" (Ex. 12: 8–11). Modern usage has adapted these biblical instructions, yet the original intent remains. As religious liturgies regularly try to bring past paradigmatic events alive in the present, so the Lord made his people pass over from slavery to freedom "this night."

The festivals for harvest and ingathering had the interesting feature of requiring Israelite males to journey to Jerusalem, the capital city where the Temple was, to present themselves to the Lord. That provided for a regular return to the center of Israelite existence, and it recalled the form of Israel's existence in the desert, when the tribes, numbered according to their males, regularly assembled before the Lord, who was leading them in cloud by day and pillar of fire by night.

The high holy days of the Fall, which include the New Year and the Day of Atonement, are the peak of the Jewish religious calendar. Leo Trepp has expressed the traditional Jewish regard for these days as follows:

"Fall marks *Rosh Hashanah,* the Beginning of the Year, New Year's Day. 'On the first of [the month of] Tishri the calendar year begins' (Mishnah Rosh Hashanah 1:1). The opening period of the year is a time of great solemnity, sober judgment, and awesome awareness of God's power. It is a period of repentance, of return to God, of renewal. These are the Yamin [sic] Norain [sic], the Days of Awe.

"Pious tradition linked this moment of renewal with the supposed date of the creation of the world; it must be a creative moment in the building of a better world. The Days of Awe open with the festival of Rosh Hashanah, followed by a week of repentance (when in daily pursuits

Jews are bidden to put into action the resolutions they have made). They culminate in Yom Kippur, the Day of Atonement, when—in complete separation from the world, united with God for a full period of a night and day—Jews confess their shortcomings and ask for forgiveness, not only of God but equally of their fellows, and return to daily living with new confidence and a new purpose."[10]

The other Jewish festivals, such as Hanukkah (commemorating the dedication of the Maccabees, liberators of Israel from pagan Greek power) and Simhat Torah (following the last day of Sukkot, when the cycle of readings from the Torah ends and begins again, causing Jews to celebrate the joy that Torah gives), have helped to punctuate the year with occasions to remember high points in the history of the covenanted people or special foci of covenantal life. The festivals, like the tractates of the Talmud, could become absorbing matters for study. Religious people regularly develop the ability to invest a given celebration with overtones of the entirety of their faith. Thus any of the holidays could focus the light of the whole, like the facet of a diamond. In the joy bestowed by the Torah, for example, pious Jews could find an epitome of all the Lord's benefactions and all the reasons it was so great a privilege to be a Jew.

Rituals for the life-cycle also have been important, helping to pace the individual through the years and to remind the community of the passages its members were undergoing. Thus the ritual for circumcision (*bris*) not only welcomes a new male member but occasions also the recall of the covenant established with Abraham and sealed by the excision of the foreskin. In recent years many Jewish congregations have developed parallel rituals for welcoming a new female member into the community. Typically, the celebration of a new birth brings family and friends together for good food, drink, and conversation. It marks a happy time, in which the overtones of religious faith and social solidarity flowed into and out from one another.

The ritual for coming of age (*bar mitzvah*) usually has been celebrated at age thirteen. Thenceforth the young male is accounted an adult, as his reading of the Torah symbolizes. To be subject to Torah, privileged to study Torah, learned in Torah, and the like, has been the traditional badge of Jewish adulthood. (For that reason, rituals for calling girls to read from the Torah and celebrating girls' maturation have developed in recent years). When one inquires into the remarkable Jewish love of learning and proficiency in learning, this connection to Torah stands out as a primary cause. Nothing has been more honored than mastery of the holy Law, and it has been easy to transfer such honor to respect for learning in general. The study of Torah in rabbinical schools has been a vigorous, dialectical process, with students pushing one another to greater feats of memory, analysis, and interpretation. At each Jewish festival, each service in the synagogue, Torah has ruled at center stage. The ceremony for bar mitzvah (taking on the responsibilities of obeying the precepts of the Torah) therefore can epitomize the aspirations of adult Jewish life.

Marriage has been a joyous time, when the command to increase, be fruitful, and multiply has come into special focus. Judaism has hallowed marriage and considered it the most desirable state. Children have represented the bounty of the Lord, and the continuance of the covenanted people. Some Jewish mystical speculation has placed marital love in the depths of divinity itself, making the romance between the marital partners a symbol of the divine creativity. Standing under the *huppah*, the wedding canopy, the couple married in a traditional Jewish wedding has completed the marriage contract and had their love blessed sevenfold, to the acclamation of the community of onlookers.

The traditional ritual for death includes a confession of sins and affirmation of faith, to prepare the dying person to meet the Lord. The deceased have been placed on the earth (in token of their return to the dust from which they had come), washed, placed in the white garments suitable for penance, placed in a simple wooden coffin, and buried to the recitation of the *kaddish*. The family of the deceased receives condolences for seven days and mourns for a month (except for parents, who are to be mourned a full year), mainly by attending synagogue and reciting the *kaddish*. The family should suspend mourning on the sabbath, lest they mar its joy, but the death functions for all whom it touches as a reminder of the frailty of life and the constant need for God's blessings.

CHRISTIAN REFLECTIONS

In dealing with Jewish prayer, Christians are well advised to appreciate two things. First, the prayer of Israel is the matrix from which Christian prayer arose, and much in later Jewish devotion expresses sentiments Christians should find instructive. Second, Judaism continued to develop after the period when Christianity arose and departed from it, creating a wealth of devotions and insights about prayer that deserve great respect.

Christianity claims to be a monotheism, just as Judaism and Islam are. In all three cases, "monotheism" ideally names a profound awareness of the fact that the living God cannot be captured by any ideas, images, or categories. The living God is the ultimate source of all beings, ideas, images, and categories. At the depths of the human spirit, the borders of the human mind, this God beckons as the definer of humanity, of creation, of possibility. Worship and prayer ideally are grateful responses to the only God, the sole Maker of heaven and earth, humanity's best hope for salvation. Worshipers use words and images, because they must, yet this consequence of their embodiment ought not to mislead them. God is beyond all words, nearer than all words, more original than the first flashes of light from which any word proceeds. To love the originality of God, the primordial being of God, is to open one's soul to the order that monotheism holds out. Such order, often expressed negatively as opposition to idolatry, pivots from the realization that only God can be the center of reality. Therefore, only God can be the center of a sane, healthy, rightly ordered human personality. Those who do not put the living God—the mysterious creativity and finality at work in every outreach of human awareness toward truth, beauty, or goodness—at the center of their lives become disordered. Inevitably, they multiply their sufferings, just as they would if they threw out their back or had an arm wrenched from its socket.

What is peculiar to Christianity is the focus of this monotheism on Jesus the Christ. The Incarnation that Christianity says does not compromise monotheism sacramentalizes the human perception of divinity. Whereas any creature reflects its divine source (since the creature is not divine and could not stand forth from nothingness apart from God's grant of being), for Christian faith human flesh has become a privileged reflection. Indeed, the flesh assumed by God from the Virgin Mary became the substantial presence of divinity in space and time. When God expressed the divine being and love in the Incarnation, people could see and hear, could touch and smell, what God was like in human terms. Much of this was very mysterious. The Incarnation did not reveal God's being or intentions in prosaic, matter-of-fact terms. Jesus struggled to understand the implications of his expressing God's revelatory and redemptive intentions, and through the centuries each generation of his followers has had to struggle in his wake. But the orthodox among his followers have hewed to the line that when the Word of God, the inner self-expression of God, took flesh and dwelt in human beings' midst, something both axial and helical occurred. Jesus represented a new plotting for history, a new backbone and nervous system, and an elevation that took history beyond what previously it was able to intend. Thus the spiral of history, its linear corkscrewing, angled upwards in ascent, becoming a helix that bores into the fullness of God's heavenly existence.

We may omit the further variations on monotheism and worship that the Christian doctrine of the Trinity introduces, lest we wander astray from our main topic. When Christians consider Jewish prayer, they are likely to feel the absence of the incarnational, sacramental qualities consequent on their own praying to a divinity become flesh. This missing feature will be noticed most acutely by those Christians whose prayer centers in the eucharist, where the enfleshment of divinity has the motif of nourishing people's spirits. However, all the Christian communities that stress the union between Christ and his members, whether in the Pauline figure of the Body of Christ or the Johannine figure of the branches joined to the vine, will think about their worship as that of a people made partakers of the divine nature, who are intimate sharers of God's own life, which is an undying love.

One might say that Jewish prayer offers Christians a salutary reminder of who the God become flesh, offering divinization, continues to be—the awesome Master of the Universe. Yet saying that could assume that Christians were so deeply immersed in the incarnational character of their own faith and worship, indeed of their own being, that they were in danger of forgetting the awesomeness of their Creator and Lord. Such does not seem to be the case. Few Christians have penetrated the revolutionary implications of the Incarnation, so few think of themselves in the first instance as members of Christ's own living Body, conduits of God's own undying love. The fact seems to be that most Christians appreciate neither the awesome implications of the small word "God" nor the shocking nearness, corporeality, and passion that the awesome God has chosen to take on.

It is interesting, and perhaps consoling, to observe the analogous dialectic suggested in Jewish prayer. For while Judaism does not believe in an incarnate Logos, a Word and Son of the eternal Lord taking flesh, it does believe in the nearness of divinity. The same God who is transcendent, never captured by creation, is writing a new covenant in human beings' hearts. For the Jewish masters of prayer, the human spirit communes with the divine Spirit, while the travails of history can be interpreted as the labors of God to bring all the peoples of the earth to his salvation. Judaism therefore knows a tension between far and near, a pulse or respiration trying to coordinate God's otherness and God's familiarity. Inevitably it focuses much of this knowledge on the everyday, the historical, the here-and-now. After all, it knows that the Lord only reveals his name to the chosen people as they sojourn with him through time (Exodus 3:14). Thus one can say that much of what Christians ought to feel about the world, their God, and themselves by virtue of the Incarnation has traced parallel patterns for Jews. Social justice, for example, has riveted the consciences of many Jews. The arts and sciences, primary expressions of human beings' responses to intimations of the divine beauty and meaning in space and time, have received strong Jewish support. Jews themselves will have to say how successfully the prayer of the typical Jewish home or synagogue has nourished such commitment to serving God in the world. It is clear, though, that the Jewish festivals and rituals for the life-cycle can shine a brilliant light on what

Jewish history and Jewish interpretation of personal existence ought to mean. Probably they ought to mean, at least in important part, that God continues to be the God of the Exodus, the God who keeps faith with the covenant, the God whose Torah is not a path out of the world so much as a path through the world. If the Exodus is a primary paradigm, then no human situation, not even that of Jews trapped in concentration camps, has ever been hopeless. If the Torah is not a call to escape but to deep immersion in God's presence, then revelation ought to disclose how the world can be beautiful, as well as what the world's ugliness and suffering mean.

Under the friendly pressure of admirable Jewish faith and prayer, the anomaly of Christians' fleeing the world, abdicating responsibility for their patch of space and time, or fearing their flesh becomes quite striking. Certainly, Jews and Christians alike know why the Bible says believers have on earth no lasting city, why believers should never put their trust in princes. The "world" is an ambiguous place, in many ways revolting from God, resisting God's calls to friendship, God's overtures of love. The closer we get to God, the better we see how we and the world are warped by sin, which we better realize is disorder, non-being, and lovelessness. Still, Jewish love of the world, Jewish fidelity to history, ought to remind Christians of their incarnate Lord. In the first place, such a reminder may spotlight the passion of Christ, which continues in his Body. The Christian Lord was despised and rejected, a man of sorrows, acquainted with grief. In anguish, he has asked each year, "My people, what have I done to you? In what way have I offended you? Answer me!" History is not pretty. Christian prayer that does not contend with the Christ bloodied for our offenses, crucified in accusation of our stupidity and sin, remains superficial.

In the second place, however, the resurrection of Christ restructures even Christ's own challenging questions. Granting peace, stabilizing joy, and demonstrating how God's weakness was stronger than human sin, the risen Christ makes the revelations of human depravity bearable. We may still see hearts of darkness, but there is a further vision, if we are willing to drop our self-sufficiency. Like a new creation, the Spirit broods in our depths, making to God an acceptable prayer. We cannot understand how God could take over our inmost being without ousting our individuality, and yet the saints make it clear that when the Spirit prays to God in human hearts the most signal humanity eventuates.

On both sides, then, God is too much for us. On that, Jewish and Christian prayer can agree. We do not plumb anything like the depths of our distance from God, and the heights of what God has prepared for those who love him far exceed our vision. Our prayer, whether silent or babbling, takes us into this fuller reality, where we are always over our heads and bedazzled. So perhaps we slowly learn that everything really is grace, a gratuity we shall never master and so would do better simply to appreciate, blessing the name of the Lord from whom it comes and continually offering him thanksgiving.

Chapter 3

ISLAM

BACKGROUND

Muslims believe that Islam expresses the genuine religion of all human beings throughout history, inasmuch as submission ("islam") to God (Allah) is religion's heart. What Allah had aroused in Adam, Abraham, Moses, and Jesus, God brought to fulfillment through revelations to Muhammad. Muhammad therefore is the "seal" of the prophecy that Allah has used to reveal the divine nature and will throughout history. The Qur'an ("Recital") containing the prophecy given to Muhammad has existed with Allah eternally and is the divine Word literally. Though secular historians tend to think that Muhammad adapted ideas that had come into Arabia through Jews and Christians, devout Muslims tend to think that Islam was a new creation: the religion specific to the Arab people, as well as the full expression of the submission crucial to all proper dealings with Allah.

Muhammad (570–632 C.E.) grew up an orphaned member of a Meccan clan. While working for a caravan company owned by a wealthy widow, Khadija, he showed enough promise for relatives to arrange his marriage to her. Some years after this, when Muhammad was about forty, he began receiving revelations. He had grown accustomed to spending time in solitude outside of Mecca, thinking about deep matters, but the revelations, mediated by an awesome figure later identified as the angel Gabriel, frightened him. Buoyed by the support of Khadija, Muhammad gradually accepted the possibility that Allah was calling him to prophesy to the Arab people. The message he felt obliged to preach stressed the sole divinity of Allah and the nearness of divine judgment.

At first Muhammad's fellow Meccans rejected his message, in good part because it would have upset their comfortable polytheism. Mecca was a crossroads for trade, and local businesses turned a good profit by selling amulets, trinkets, and other articles believed to ward off evil influences and attract benevolent powers. Muhammad left Mecca for Yathrib (Medina) in 622, drawn by a call to establish a Muslim regime there. His strongest supporters, Khadija and an uncle, had died in 619, so the call to Medina brought him out of a dark hour. Muslims date their calendar from the *hegira,* Muhammad's move to Medina in 622, because from that time a true Islam arose, blending religious and secular rule. By 630 Muhammad had returned to Mecca in triumph, having won numerous military victories against considerable odds. In the last two years of his life he further developed his ideas about the Muslim commonwealth and prepared the way for the astonishing spread of Islam that began shortly after his death.

In the years 636–640, Muslims conquered Damascus, Jerusalem, Egypt, and Persia. By 800 Muslims ruled the southern Mediterranean from Palestine to the Atlantic, as well as Afghanistan, Armenia, Iraq, and Eastern India. With the military conquests came a strong incentive for local populations to convert to Islam. Arab civilization flowered, as the arts and sciences gained wealthy patrons. Until about 1050 Muslims expanded into Europe, gaining control of most of southern Europe. North Africa was securely Muslim, and Islamic power — military, economic, and cultural — ruled the Middle East. By the end of the eleventh century, however, Muslim culture had begun to decline, though Muslim power continued to radiate from Egypt, Turkey, Arabia, and India. Skirmishes with Christian crusaders and Huns were troublesome, and the various Sufi brotherhoods complicated religion by introducing an otherworldly mysticism; however, until the advent of the rise of European powers in the sixteenth century Islam was more dominant than subjugated. Throughout modernity Muslims have been on the defensive, *historical Summary* (handwritten)

both militarily and culturally. Much of the strong feeling manifest in the recent resurgence of Islam amounts to satisfaction at success in throwing off Western control.

The gist of Islamic belief is contained in the profession of faith: There is no God but Allah, and Muhammad is Allah's prophet. Muslims are strong monotheists, convinced that only Allah rules creation. It is unthinkable that Allah would share divinity or rule with other deities. Idolatry—granting what belongs only to Allah to someone or something else—is the worst sin, and Muslims understand monotheism to deny the Christian Trinity and Incarnation. Nonetheless, Judaism and Christianity are kindred faiths, because they arose from early, imperfect revelations conveyed through the line of prophecy that culminated in Muhammad. As "people of the book," Jews and Christians might have discovered the fulfillment of their faiths in Muhammad and Islam, and they retain a special dignity.

The Qur'an (4:136) includes as articles of faith—besides Allah and Muhammad—Allah's angels, books, and messengers, as well as the Last Day. The angels have myriad functions, mediating between Allah and the world. The Qur'an is the premier book, but the Bible also has merit. Allah's messengers, such as Abraham and Jesus, are the forerunners of Muhammad. The Last Day is the day of judgment, when Allah will separate those who merit the Garden from those who merit the Fire. Human beings have a great dignity, for they are made in the image of Allah and represent his rule on earth.[1]

The great significance of these creedal convictions has been Muslims' profound appreciation of the sovereignty of Allah. Allah is the Lord of the Worlds, the complete controller of nature, history, and destiny. Islam certainly has considered human beings free and so responsible for their actions, but it has loved the rule of Allah and steadily praised his control. Only if Allah were willing would a given course of action come to fruition. Only if Allah wished would anyone prosper or decline. If fatalism was the danger in this attitude, the beneficiary was Muslims' sense of providence. Nothing occurred without Allah's agreement, so all things were in good hands.

The five "pillars" in which Islam has summarized its practice have included the confession of faith ("There is no God but

5 pillars (handwritten)

Allah, and Muhammad is his prophet"), prayer five times a day, fasting during the month of Ramadan, giving alms, and making a pilgrimage to Mecca. Muslim prayer has drawn heavily on the Qur'an and stresses praise of Allah. Traditionally Muslims face Mecca when praying. They kneel, bow, and touch their heads to the floor. Assembled in the mosque, they move in unison, standing, kneeling, and bowing together. Usually men and women are separated, and women's access to both the mosque and the Qur'an has varied through the ages, but women are equally obliged to pray.

Fasting during the month of Ramadan is both a penance, to purify body and spirit, and a celebration. Ideally one takes no food or drink during the daylight hours but rejoices after dark. On the whole Islam is not an ascetic religion, though numerous Sufis and mystics have been ascetics. Still, each year Ramadan offers a reminder of the surpassing value of pleasing Allah and the transient character of all this-worldly pleasures.

Giving alms is not an optional matter of purely personal charity. It reflects Muhammad's deep instinct that Islam ought to make men and women brothers and sisters. In Muhammad's day a clan structure sometimes separated Arabs and divided society, leaving many cracks through which the poor might fall into neglect. The Prophet wanted Islam to become the basis for a new solidarity, and giving alms became a practical way to express Muslims' kinship. The amount of the alms has varied from time to time and place to place, but two to three percent of one's annual income has been a rough target.

The fifth pillar, the pilgrimage to Mecca, has loomed as a high point of each Muslim's life. If at all possible, at least once during one's life one is to visit the birthplace of Islam and experience both the sanctity of the Islamic origins and the catholicity of the membership of the House of Islam. During the periods designated for pilgrimage, visitors to Mecca wear a simple style of clothing that disguises their ethnic and economic differences. They perform standard, ritualized prayers, visit memorable sites, and contemplate the black stone of the Kaaba, the inner precinct of the Meccan holy space. Recalling the experiences of Abraham and Muhammad, they feel the grand history of their tradition. Regularly, Muslim pilgrims report that making the *hajj* to Mecca has flooded them with joy.

Nowadays Islam is the world's fastest growing religion. By some estimates Muslims now number nearly one billion adherents, and now Islam has a presence on all continents. In addition to its traditional base in the Near East, Islam now is especially strong in Africa, Pakistan, Afghanistan, the Eastern U.S.S.R., Indonesia, and Malaysia. The majority of Muslims are Sunnis, adherents to the group that has thought leadership in the community need not be tied to the Prophet's bloodline. Shiites, who have thought community leadership ought to repose in descendants of Muhammad, have been strongest in Persia/Iran. While Sunnis and Shiites differ on significant details and sometimes show considerable animosity toward one another, they share the substantials of faith, practice, and legal codes. For all Muslims Muhammad represents the ideal Muslim life and Fatima, the Prophet's daughter, is a model of Muslim femininity. Everywhere Islam retains the ideal of fusing religion and general culture, admitting little if any distinction between the secular and the sacred. Everywhere a heritage of high achievement in poetry, architecture, mathematics, astronomy, warfare, and mysticism prods Muslims toward cultural renovation. Nowadays fundamentalism is a powerful force, but traditionally Muslims have been sophisticated exegetes and lawyers. Fundamentalist or sophisticate, however, every committed Muslim believes deeply in prayer.

STORIES

Consider the commitment to prayer and mastering the Qur'an suggested by the following scene from a novel about a Muslim childhood in Senegal:

At a sign from the teacher, the boy had put away his writing tablet. But he did not move from where he was sitting. He was engrossed in a scrutiny of his schoolmaster, whom he now saw in profile. The man was old, emaciated, withered and shrunken by mortifications of the flesh. He used never to laugh. The only moments of enthusiasm that could be seen in him were those in which, lost in his mystic meditations or listening to the recital of the Word of God, he would stand erect, all tense, and seem to be lifted from the earth, as if raised by some inner force. There were many times, on the other hand, when, driven to a frenzied rage by the laziness or the blunders of one of his pupils, he would give himself up to outrageously brutal outbreaks of violence. But these outbreaks of violence were factors in, expressions of, the interest he took in the disciple who was at fault. The more he held him in esteem, the wilder were his rages. . . . The teacher was from several points of view a formidable man. Two occupations filled his life: the work of the spirit and the work of the field. To the work of the field he devoted the strict minimum of his time, and he demanded from the earth no more than he had to have for his extremely frugal nourishment and that of his family, not including his pupils. The rest of his days and nights he consecrated to study, to meditation, to prayer, and to the education and molding of the young people who had been confided to his care.[2]

The novelist creating this autobiographical scene intended it to be part of a general description of what life had been like in traditional Muslim Africa, before promising youths like himself encountered Western modernity in such centers of higher learning as Paris. Traditional life had been steeped in a sense of God, the Lord of the Worlds whose presence pervaded nature and glistened in the words of the Qur'an. At sunrise and sunset, one could feel the touch of the Creator. By immersing oneself in the divine Word, which was the crux of the traditional education, one could fuse with the means Allah had created to reveal himself. The traditional African Muslim culture was holistic, everything finding its niche because correlated with Allah. It developed a rich, thick, three-dimensional appreciation of beauty and meaning. The little boy pictured in the story gained considerable sophistication when, as a young man, he studied in Paris, but the novelist is more interested in the boy's losses. The painful paradox seemed to be that to come of age and enter the modern world, the boy had to surrender a considerably more satisfying heritage. Once the wholeness of the world he had known as a child was fractured, the novelist realized he could never put either it or himself back together.

The potential of the apparently simple recitation of the Qur'an and bowing to Allah that has filled mosques and Muslim lives for centuries therefore has been profound. Many might merely go through the motions, accepting the social conventions, but some were taken to their depths. The many Muslim mystics witness to the thirst for union with God that Islamic prayer has nurtured and fulfilled. The Sufi conviction that genuine religion would fill the feelings and water the soul penetrated many Muslim precincts. If the surface of Muslim culture seems formidably dominated by religious law, the depths seem as profound as the spirit's journeys into the endlessness of Allah.

Muhammad has served Muslims as the model of prayer, as well as the model of action to forward Islam. Describing Muhammad's prayer, Michael Cook has stressed how Qur'anic revelation advanced his initial searches for Allah and made daily prayer a staple of Muslim piety:

how to prayer began

> Eventually Muhammad was given his prophetic mission. He had been in the habit of spending one month of each year on the nearby Mount Hira. This, it would seem, was a religious custom of pagan times; while there, he might be joined by his family and would feed such of the poor as came to him. One night while he was residing on the mountain in this fashion the angel Gabriel visited him in his sleep, and ordered him to recite; in response to Muhammad's puzzlement he then taught him a passage of the 96th chapter of the Koran, which appropriately begins with the command, 'recite!'. The experience was in two ways characteristic of what followed: Gabriel was to be the normal channel of communication between God and Muhammad, and it was in such fragments that what was to become the Muslim scripture, the Koran, was gradually revealed to him. ... After receiving his mission, Muhammad spent fifteen (or thirteen, or ten) years in Mecca. During this period the episodic revelation of scripture continued, and a simple ritual and morality were developed. The ritual consisted of a number (fixed at five) of daily prayers, to be

performed in a state of ritual purity attained by washing;
the practical details were demonstrated to Muhammad by
Gabriel. The morality comprised such principles as ab-
staining from theft and fornication. This was also the time
when Muhammad was vouchsafed a remarkable supernatural journey. One night while he was sleeping in the sanctuary in Mecca, he was taken by Gabriel to Jerusalem;
there he met Abraham, Moses, and Jesus, and led them
in prayer, after which he was taken on a visit to heaven.
His subsequent description of the layout of Jerusalem was
confirmed, presumably from personal experience, by one
of his followers.[3]

Muhammad's prayer therefore sometimes was miraculous.
The revelations that came to him through the mediation of Gabriel (though sometimes in the Qur'an the voice speaking seems
to be that of Allah himself) riveted his imagination as well as
his soul. Muhammad saw visions and heard commands. Ordinary
Muslims might consider their prayer mainly the fulfillment of
the command of Allah, but the example of Muhammad framed
all prayer as a place where Allah might communicate his will
dramatically.
The night journey of Muhammad to Jerusalem has been a
favorite subject of what portraiture Islam has allowed. Some of
the Persian miniaturists, for example, have showed the Prophet
being carried to Jerusalem and heaven. The tradition of the
journey helped to cement the ties between Muhammad, Abraham, and Jesus. Only Mecca and Medina are holier to Muslims
than Jerusalem, and the mosque known as the Dome of the
Rock, to the east of the Western Wall in Jerusalem, commemorates both the rock on which Abraham was to sacrifice Isaac
and Muhammad's journey.
The ritual purity that Muhammad considered prayer to require was part of the religious culture of his day and has remained significant in Islam. Outside the typical mosque is a
water fountain and those entering the mosque to pray are expected not only to remove their shoes but also to wash themselves. Like Judaism, Islam has considered contact with God to

require physical purity (and has considered menstruation an impurity).

A story about the Prophet suggests how Muslims have thought his prayer made him an oracle of wisdom and a familiar of angels:

why pray

"A man asked the Prophet, 'What is faith?' He replied, 'Faith consists of belief in God, His angels, the meeting with Him, His Apostles, and the resurrection.' The man said, 'What is *islam*? He replied, '*Islam* consists of the service of God, the refusal to associate anything with him, prayer, almsgiving, and fasting during the month of Ramadan.'

"The man said, 'What does it mean to do good?' He replied, 'To serve God as though you could see Him. Even though you cannot see Him, He can see you.' The man said, 'When is the last hour?' He replied, 'The one who is asked does not know any more than he who asks, but I can tell you about the signs that point to it. When the slavewoman gives birth to her master, that is one of the signs. When the naked and the barefoot become chiefs of the people, that is one of the signs. When the shepherds take insolent pride in constructing buildings, that is one of the signs. Then there are five things only God knows.' After that he recited, 'Surely God—He has knowledge of the Hour; He sends down the rain; He knows what is in the wombs. No soul knows what it shall earn tomorrow, and no soul knows in what land it shall die. Surely God is All-Knowing, All-Aware.'

"The man then slipped away. The Apostle of God said, 'Send that man back to me.' They tried to do so, but they could not find him. The Apostle of God said, 'It was Gabriel who came to teach the people their religion.' "[4]

Because the Qur'an had come from God, and presently existed as God's Word, the Qur'an could mediate not only God's wisdom and will but also God's presence. Steeped in the Qur'an, Muhammad taught and ruled as though inspired. What he had received from God came to his lips when people asked about faith or practice. The barrier between his prayer and his teaching or action was slight. His life seemed to realize the ideal of finding God in all things. Later Muslim spirituality spoke of the Qur'an and nature as the twin fonts of revelation. The example of the Prophet led many of his followers to think that prayer could reveal God's presence everywhere. Thus the stories about Muhammad created the view that waging war, making love, or passing decisions on community problems was not only compatible with prayer but a mode of serving Allah quite like prayer. For those immersed in the Qur'an, formed by God's Word, nothing was profane. Islam could be a submission to a Lord found everywhere.

PRAYERS

The traditional Muslim has learned about prayer from earliest childhood. Writing about female spirituality in Islam, Saadia Khawar Khan Chishti has said, "... a spiritual mother nurtures the soul of her child with the powerful effect of the recitation of the *Shahadah,* the oft-repeated prayer (*Surat al-fatihah*), and the beautiful Names or Attributes of God by singing them as a lullaby for putting the child to sleep or for comforting a wailing or a disturbed child. In doing so, the mother makes her contribution in permeating the very being of the child with the most powerful words of the Qur'an."[5]

The *Shahadah* is the creed: There is no Allah but Allah, and Muhammad is Allah's prophet. The "oft-repeated prayer" is the opening surah of the Qur'an: "In the name of Allah, the Compassionate, the Merciful. Praise be to Allah, the Lord of Creation, the Compassionate, the Merciful, King of Judgement Day! You alone we worship, and to You alone we pray for help. Guide us to the straight path, the path of those whom You have favoured, not of those who have incurred Your wrath, nor of those who have gone astray."[6] Concerning the beautiful names of Allah, G. D. Newby has written, "Allah was for Muhammad the only reality, the Truth, the Creator, the Sustainer, the Possessor, the Destroyer, the Redeemer, who has all power and might. Allah is the Seer, the Knower, the Hearer, the Wise. These epithets, or 'names' as they are often called in Islam, are found throughout the Qur'an as seeming definitions, though it would appear that in defining God Muhammad was more concerned as a prophet than as a theologian. Some ninety-nine descriptions, not all derived directly from the Qur'an, are known in later Islam as the 'ninety-nine beautiful names of Allah.' "[7]

The Qur'an is organized so that its surahs appear roughly in order of their length. After the first surah, quoted above, which has a unique status, comes the longest surah, traditionally called "the Cow." The last three surahs (112–114) illustrate how the Qur'an is seldom more than a step away from prayer: "In the Name of Allah, the Compassionate, the Merciful. Say: 'Allah is One, the Eternal God. He begot none, nor was He begotten. None is equal to Him.' " (112) "In the name of Allah, the Compassionate, the Merciful. Say: 'I seek refuge in the Lord of Daybreak from the mischief of His creation; from the mischief of the night when she spreads her darkness; from the mischief of conjuring witches; from the mischief of the envier, when he envies.' " (113) "In the Name of Allah, the Compassionate, the Merciful. Say: 'I seek refuge in the Lord of Men, the King of Men, the God of men, from the mischief of the slinking prompter who whispers in the hearts of men; from jinn [evil spirits] and men.' " (114)

Muslim prayer (*salat*) is, as noted, one of the five pillars of Islamic faith. Two other terms, *du'a* and *dhikr,* are used to focus respectively on supplication and remembrance of Allah. Muslims are supposed to pray five times a day: at dawn, noon, the afternoon, sunset, and night. Before each period of prayer they should purify themselves by washing their face, hands, head, and feet. They should also cleanse their mouth, nose, and teeth. During these ablutions it is customary to petition God according to set prayers. For example, after washing the feet one prays, "O God! Make firm my feet on the Path on the day when they easily slip on it."[8] Failing water, one may use sand for purification. After seminal emission or menstruation one ought to take a full bath. Those praying should be well covered, males at least from the navel to the knees and females completely, except for the face, hands, and feet. The place of worship need not be a mosque (females usually are not allowed in the mosque with men and pray at home) but it should be clean. One ought to face in the direction of Mecca (each mosque has a niche —*qib-lah*—indicating this direction). Generally the times of prayer are announced by the call of a muezzin (cryer), who traditionally cried from the minaret atop the mosque. A session of prayer generally includes bows (the number varying according to the time of the prayer—for example, two at dawn but four at noon). After the bows, those praying tend to stand in straight rows behind the leader (*imam*), whom they follow. Those praying should speak just after the leader and quietly, so that only the leader's voice is audible. One may pray alone, however.

The Qur'an contains verses traditionally accounted the prayers of prophets or saints. Thus surah 17:80 has been considered a prayer given to Muhammad: "O my Lord, let security and truth precede and follow me wherever You lead me. Let authority and succor from Your presence be with me." Surah 11:41 has been considered a prayer of Noah: "In God's name be the course and the mooring: let us embark." Abraham and his father are credited with the prayer in surah 60:4–5: "Our Lord, in You we have trusted. To you we have turned in penitence. Yours is our final destiny. Lord, ever mighty and wise, let us give no occasion to the enemies of truth, but forgive us." Moses is credited with surah 20:25–28: "O my Lord, enlarge my heart and facilitate the task I face. Take the stammer from my speech that they may understand what I tell them."[9]

Because the Qur'an was digested so thoroughly, many Muslims used verses such as these in accommodated senses. The embarking of Noah might stand for the beginning of any new venture. The forgiveness sought by Abraham and his father might apply to any transgression.

A venerable prayer for the days of Ramadan, during which Muslims are to fast, stresses the forgiveness sought during the fast:

"O my God, the petitioners stand before Thy gate, and the needy seek refuge in Thy courts. The ship of the wretched stands on the shore of the ocean of Thy grace and goodness, seeking passage into the presence of Thy mercy and compassion. O my God, if in this blessed month Thou forgivest only those whose fasting and performance is right, who will take the part of the transgressor who defaults, when he perishes in the sea of his sins and transgression? O my God, if Thou are merciful only towards the obedient, who will take the part of the rebellious? If Thou receivest only those who have done well, then what of those who have fallen short? O my God, those who fast have surely gained, the faithful doers have victory and the sincere are delivered. But we, Thy guilty servants, have mercy upon us out of Thy compassion. Liberate us from damnation by Thy pardon; forgive us our trespasses with the rest of the believers, men and women, through Thy mercy, O Thou most faithful."[10]

This prayer for Ramadan expresses the traditional Muslim stance toward Allah. The believer is always a petitioner, even a slave. So surpassing is the power and overseeing of Allah that the revelation of the divine compassion and mercy is a tremendous grace. Had Allah not chosen to be merciful, none would have survived. The refrain of this prayer for Ramadan begging Allah to accept those who have not kept the fast blamelessly brings out the Islamic understanding of grace. Muslims have not held a doctrine of original sin, such as that implied in the Jewish and Christian understandings of Genesis. But Muslims have considered human beings to be weak and forgetful. The majesty of Allah is such that no human being could ever attain righteousness in a strict sense. The practice of *dhikr* (remembrance) grew among the Sufis to help Muslims recall the presence of Allah and so be less forgetful of the divine majesty. Seeing and knowing all, Allah is ever-present to the believer. Much of the believer's progress in sanctity consists in taking this constant divine presence to heart.

The Sufi program produced many eminent teachers and mystics. Many of the techniques associated with Sufi prayer amounted to helping believers immerse themselves in the mental world created by the Qur'an. The Sufi masters described the different stages on the journey to union with God, but the stages were less important than the general prescription to remember God's presence and goodness. Indeed, some of the Sufi masters moved beyond the usual presentation of Allah, which stressed the divine Lordship, to speak of divine love. For example, the following classical text makes the love of God the goal of pious devotions:

" 'Nothing is more pleasing to Me, as a means for My slave to draw near unto Me, than worship which I have made binding upon him; and My slave ceaseth not to draw near unto Me with added devotions of his free will until I love him; and when I love him I am the Hearing wherewith he heareth and the Sight wherewith he seeth and the Hand whereby he graspeth and the Foot whereon he walketh.' The whole of Sufism—its aspirations, its practice, and in a sense also even its doctrine—is summed up in this Holy Tradition, which is quoted by the Sufis perhaps more often than any other text apart from the Qur'an. As may be inferred from it, their practices are of two kinds: rites which are binding on all Muslims, and additional voluntary rites. When a novice enters an order, one of the first things he or she has to do is to acquire an extra dimension which will confer a depth and a height on rites which (assuming an Islamic upbringing) have been performed more or less exoterically since childhood."[11]

In other words, for the Sufis such prescribed duties as the five pillars became rituals to be interiorized. The Sufis' goal was to make the five daily prayers, the fast during Ramadan, and the other duties devotions springing from the heart. The "exoteric" execution of the ordinary believer stayed at the level of physical performance. The Sufis thought all such devotions had the potential to unite the believer with Allah, so that eventually there would be no separation between disciple and Lord.

RITUALS

Islam has fostered numerous rituals, as the indication that Muslims usually have bowed a certain number of times for a given hour of prayer and washed themselves in specific ways before prayer suggests. The point to Muslim ritual generally is to induce states of soul conducive to hearing the Word of Allah and having one's submission improved by it. In the mosque, during Ramadan, while on pilgrimage, and at other significant moments, Muslims have employed traditions about how the Prophet acted or an ancestor such as Abraham behaved to ritualize their behavior. A story about the processions associated with the pilgrimage to Mecca illustrates the weight of tradition.

Once the great-grandson of the Prophet, Ali b. al-Husayn, was circumambulating a shrine at Mecca when a man approached and asked to question him. Ali kept silent until he had finished his religious walk and then invited the man to ask his question. The question was how the custom of circumambulation had arisen. Ali asked the questioner where he dwelt and, learning that he dwelt in Jerusalem, whether he had read the "two books," meaning the Torah of the Jews and the Gospel of the Christians. Hearing that the man had, Ali then explained that the custom of circumambulation went back to when Allah had told the angels that He was going to appoint a human being his vice-gerent on earth. The angels protested that this decision would only bring corruption and bloodshed. In their opinion, Allah would have been wiser to appoint an angel to rule upon earth. Whereupon Allah told them that he knew something they did not, which they took as a rebuke. In fear that they had offended Allah, they went to the divine throne, made signs of humility, and went in a circuit around the throne for three hours. Looking upon them, Allah granted them mercy.

Later the Lord established a house beneath the divine throne, adorned it, and commanded the angels to circumambulate around this house rather than his throne. This was easier for them. Allah then gave the angels the commission of building on earth a house like the heavenly one. When they had completed this task, the Lord ordered all the creatures of earth to circumambulate the earthly house, just as the angels had walked around the heavenly house. That was how the custom of circumambulating the precincts of Mecca came into being. The man who had asked the question was well satisfied.

The story illustrates the Muslim tendency, shared with many other religions, to ground religious customs in heavenly archetypes. What occurs below, here on earth, ought to reflect what occurs above, in heaven. Ideally, earthly life is a miniature of heavenly existence. Thus the Qur'an that the Muslim can hear, touch, and read is a replica of the Qur'an that has existed alongside God from eternity. Thus the exercises of the pilgrimage to Mecca repeat patterns laid out in heaven, where worship of Allah is unmarred.[12]

As Islam was transported to new cultural areas, outside of Arabia, it interacted with local customs. The result was that many Muslim rituals gained local color and flavor. The Yoruba Muslims of Africa, for example, have ritualized their life-cycle, putting a Muslim face on their ancient sense that each phase of a person's passage from the cradle to the grave ought to have helpful ceremonies. For example, at the time a Yoruba becomes a member of the Muslim community (on the eighth day after birth, for children, or at a formal ceremony marking their conversion, for adults), he or she receives a religious name. For adults an ablution marks the occasion, to symbolize the pure life the convert ought to be beginning. Under the direction of a presiding cleric, the new Muslims doff their old clothing, don loin cloths, and submit their hands and legs to a threefold washing. The cleric also washes their elbows, nose, and ears. At the end of the ceremony he pours water on their head and chest. The notion is that a true Muslim comes before Allah thoroughly cleansed (as also of the times of prayer). Living in the presence of Allah demands purity of both body and soul.

For marriage, another significant phase of the life-cycle, Yoruba Muslims require that the presiding cleric have certified that the prospective bride and groom seem good for one another. He also should have prayed for them. The groom has to pay money to the family of the bride and give them gifts. During the wedding ceremony the cleric asks the groom whether he takes the bride as his wife, will give her lodging, feed her, and love her. The cleric invokes the Qur'an (4:34) on the importance of marriage as a sign of Allah's care, and he asks the bride the same questions he asked the groom.

The third major phase of the Yoruba life-cycle to be ritualized is death. Hearing of a death, neighbors gather to dig a grave. They wash the corpse and repeat the ablutions proper for a convert. Before lowering the corpse into the grave, they dress it in a white cap, loin cloth, and sewn sheet. A Muslim cleric prays for the dead person, asking Allah to forgive his or her sins. The family of the deceased pays the cleric both money and food. Some families hold a memorial service eight days after the burial. The ceremony usually features readings from the Qur'an and a eulogy of the dead person.

Many Muslims celebrate such occasions as New Year's Day, which typically is a time for feasting. Some commemorations recall the exit of Noah from the ark after the flood, when he was very hungry. The birthday of the Prophet and the time of his journey to Jerusalem and paradise are other popular feast days. For the birthday of the Prophet it is customary to sponsor a display of learning. Young men who have been progressing in their studies get a chance to show off what they have mastered and children may act out scenes from the Prophet's life.

The Muslim world over, Friday is the day of special celebration, the Muslim Sabbath, when attendance at the mosque is obligatory. In addition to readings from the Qur'an the typical mosque will sponsor a sermon relating the scriptural passage for the day to the believer's life. The rest of the day ideally is a time for families to relax together. In Cairo, for example, Friday is the busiest day at the zoo. Groups such as the Yoruba, who have had a tradition of giving different days of the week special weights, have solemnized Thursday evening as the accession of Friday, much as Jews have solemnized Friday evening as the beginning of Shabbat. Many Muslims think of Wednesday as a day of blessings, which has caused Wednesday to be the most popular day for weddings. The last Wednesday of each lunar month is especially solemn, because folk religion tends to locate there the evils that each month carries (no doubt this thought is stimulated by the waning of the moon and so the greater impact of darkness). The last Wednesday of the month is the time when one may gain special blessings against death and the powers of darkness.

At the roots of the rituals of many world religions lie customs of the religious complexes that preceded them. Thus Christian rituals adapted Jewish customs and Buddhist rituals adapted Hindu customs. In the case of Islam, the Arabs who embraced Muhammad's message were often influenced by pre-Muslim Bedouin customs. Even when such customs did not receive official Muslim sanction they could remain in the background and shape popular Muslim religion. Having discussed Bedouin ideas about sacred stones and *jinn,* Joseph Henninger has said of Bedouin ideas about the dead: "It has not been sufficiently established that the dead are generally regarded as powerful, superhuman beings. They appear rather as being deprived of protection, needing the charity of the living. This is why sacrifices for the dead in general do not seem to signify a cult of the dead but rather a continuation of social obligations beyond the grave. On the other hand ancestors ... were an object of real veneration. People not only slew animals and made libations by their tombs but also erected stone structures as they did at the sanctuaries of local gods. Like the sanctuaries these graves were places of refuge."[13]

Muslim convictions depreciated the influence of the dead, seeing them as consigned by Allah to either the Fire or the Garden. Nonetheless, the tombs of the revered dead, especially of those accounted saints, have always been important in Islam and frequently have functioned as sanctuaries. Women and others on the margins of power have tended to use such sanctuaries as places where they could gather to pour out their troubles to the saint and receive some peer support. Drawing on the aura of the saint's presence, those needing help would expose their troubles. Others in attendance then regularly would console the petitioner; a solidarity in suffering might arise. The person in pain could go home relieved of the burden of carrying the worry or suffering in secret; he or she would feel consoled that others also were having to beg Allah to light their way. In fact the typical sanctuary developed ritualistic patterns designed to facilitate both prayer to the saints and communal comfort.

Despite its apparent simplicity, and its aversion to ikons and embellished worship, Islam certainly has produced effective rituals. As the law codes multiplied, many facets of daily life gained a ritualistic character. Like Judaism, Islam was concerned about diet, branding pork and alcohol unseemly. It was also concerned about deportment in the mosque, between the sexes, between teachers and students, and so on. Ideally, daily life fell into a pattern of work, prayer, and recreation at home or in the village square that ritualized most of the average Muslim's time.

ritual summary

CHRISTIAN REFLECTIONS

When Christians reflect on the Muslim experience with prayer, probably the first thing they ought to consider is the profound appreciation of the oneness of God that Muslim prayer celebrates. Allah is the sole, the only God. All divinity reposes in him. And his divinity is overwhelming: his is the force that hurled the stars to their places, that created human beings from a mere clot of blood. Allah is a powerful, majestic deity. His first name is Lord. Muslim prayer is the expression of submission to the Lord. At prayer, the Muslim above all is a creature trembling in gratitude that Allah should have shown himself compassionate and merciful, lest his power have crushed all creatures to dust.

The compassion and mercy of Allah came to a climax in the revelation of the Qur'an. As many scholars have noted, the Qur'an holds the place in Muslim faith that Christ the Incarnate Word holds in Christian faith. It is the enfleshment of the divine spirit. It is the paramount revelation of the divine will and nature. To help human beings gain the Garden and avoid the Fire, Allah communicated to Muhammad the essentials of revelation. But devout Muslims, like devout Christians, are interested in more than avoiding hellfire and gaining heaven. For them the Qur'an is most precious as a mediator of the divine presence. When the words are chanted, the divine presence becomes audible, palpable, and a matter of more intense experience.

Muhammad is not the incarnation of Allah. Muslims have always rejected attempts to divinize Muhammad. Allah is so transcendent of the world and human beings that it is unthinkable anything created could partake of his godhead. Muslim philosophers did speculate about the participation of creatures in the divine being, but their speculations did not conclude at the sort of divinization (*theosis*) that Eastern Christian speculation reached when joined to hints from Christian scripture. When Muslim mystics such as Al Hallaj ventured to proclaim themselves identified with Allah, they risked death on the charge of blasphemy. (In fact, Al Hallaj was killed.)

Just as the Muslim instinct about the oneness of God made

pantheism appear very wicked, so this instinct made the Christian doctrine of the Trinity appear untenable. Despite Christian insistence that God remained completely One, the Christian teachings about Father, Son, and Spirit were received in Islam as a tritheism: three gods. Relatedly, the Christian teachings about the divinity of Christ and the incarnation of the Logos have struck most Muslims as blasphemous. The Qur'an insists that Allah could have no partakers of his divinity and that it is unthinkable that he would have a son in the literal sense of a divine offspring.

The difference that this Muslim understanding of monotheism placed between Muslim and Christian prayer centers in mediation and iconography. Christian prayer generally has favored sacraments, reasoning that if the Word of God took flesh, then flesh is a valid and perhaps in some ways a privileged mode of contact with God. Some commentators credit the iconoclast controversy that developed in Eastern Christianity to Muslim and Jewish influences. Under the pressure of both Muslim and Jewish insistence on the transcendence of the divine, some of the Eastern emperors came to consider ikons idolatrous. When the position of the ikonodules (those favoring the veneration of ikons) won the day, Eastern Christianity implicitly asserted its distinction from Islam and Judaism. Christian worship, focused on Christ, meant a different sense of the potential of matter to reveal God and a different understanding of divine transcendence.

Christians commenting on Islam might reflect that Muslim iconoclasm has not been absolute, and that in fact no religion can be wholly opposed to ikons. Muslims have used both the Qur'an and the figure of Muhammad to focus their prayer. They have produced beautiful mosques, wonderfully adorned with nonpictorial art, as helps for prayer. Muslim rituals, as we have seen, have engaged the body and the senses. Muslim chanting of verses from the Qur'an and calligraphic beautification of Qur'ans have been outstanding arts. So one can speak of an "incarnational" principle in both Islamic theology and Islamic prayer.

As well, one can point to the ways in which the Muslim convictions about the immanence of Allah (as near as the pulse at the believer's throat) have balanced convictions about Allah's transcendence. In addition, one can underscore the Muslim conviction that nature is a revelation of God, providing a channel to supplement or precede Qur'anic revelation. The Lordship of Allah ought to be plain from the patterns of nature. The power and order one sees in nature ought to be credited to Allah. In the Garden nature will prosper just as saved human beings do. The Garden will have delightful trees and streams. Since the difference between God's sharing the divine nature and God's communicating through material things can strike the average believer as slight, those who study religions comparatively can suspect that the Islamic ban on representations of Allah did not mean that Muslims stopped trying to find ways in which the divine presence was mediated to them.

Sometimes non-Muslims have taken the Islamic denial that Muhammad was divine to mean a depreciation of the Prophet's importance. This interpretation is in error. Muslims generally have lavished great affection on the Prophet and considered upholding his honor very important. The recent controversies about the portrayal of Muhammad in the novelist Salman Rushdie's work *The Satanic Verses* illustrate the fervor of Muslim devotion to upholding the honor of the Prophet. Because Rushdie's depiction was deemed insulting, and, as one raised a Muslim, he was deemed aware of what he was doing, Muslim fury abounded. One seeking a Christian parallel would find one if insults and blasphemies were thrown at Jesus, even though Jesus differs from Muhammad in being acclaimed divine by his orthodox followers. Muslims have so identified the dignity of the Prophet with the divinity of the Lord who chose and used him that to insult the Prophet was to blaspheme against Allah.

The political overtones of the Rushdie controversy also had theological foundations and implications. Because Islam has not separated the sacred and the secular as modern Western nations have, it made sense to many Muslims to call for criminal sanctions against Rushdie. Whether the Ayatollah Khomeini went too far in demanding a death penalty and inviting an assassination, and how Muslim societies defend the rights of free speech and artistic creativity, are further issues. Suffice it to say that in a Muslim horizon what Rushdie did could plausibly seem a capital crime. To decry such a verdict on Muslim grounds, one would have to argue that neither Allah nor Muhammad is injured by offensive human speech and that the mercy of Allah suggests giving those who have blasphemed time to come to see the error of their ways.

Christians might profitably compare their own sense of the living God with that of devout Muslims and see whether their generally more casual attitude toward antireligious speech does not reflect some tepidity or indifference. This is a charge that some Christian commentators sympathetic to Muslim concerns about blasphemy have raised, and it bears notice. For our topic of prayer, the question would be whether Christianity has kept alive the sense of the divine presence that animates the best Muslim prayer. Is the grandeur of God, the majesty of God, sufficiently flourishing in Christian churches to provoke the bows, heartfelt prostrations, commitment to daily prayer, and sensitivity to affronts to the divine dignity that one finds in many parts of the Muslim world? Is the price that Christians have paid for tolerance and pluralism higher than it might have been or than most Christians have realized?

In answering these questions, perhaps Christians would be well advised to contemplate the way that their faith says God has chosen to present divinity. On both Old Testament and New Testament grounds, Christians might argue that divinity has chosen to make itself vulnerable. The figure of Hosea suffering the infidelities of his wife Gomer epitomizes the insight of the Israelite prophets into the self-abnegation of the divine love, while the Christian identification of Jesus with the Suffering Servant of Second Isaiah and the Christian stress on the divine self-emptying (*kenosis*) take such self-abnegation to the cross. Christian orthodoxy has said that on the cross God died. Because of the union of the Logos with passible flesh, the one who expired in agony was God's Son. If so, outrage at human offenses toward God have to be measured, while wonder at the reaches of the divine goodness have to be expanded.

The implication for Christian prayer would seem to be an option for images of God that express the divine compassion and long-suffering. In the parables of Jesus, especially that of the prodigal son, we see God putting aside the divine dignity and justice to let a parental love triumph. In the speech of Jesus about this parental love, and the intimacy that Jesus assumes with his Father, we see a defeat of the divine transcendence and dignity, as least inasmuch as those formidable attributes are likely to provoke fear in human imaginations. God has given us all that God had to give. God has suffered on our behalf, as though to make it impossible for us to doubt the divine love or the warrants for our trusting God completely. The result ought to be a prayer that goes to God in utter confidence, not because human beings have great beauty or justice but because God is unimaginably good.

Chapter 4

HINDUISM

BACKGROUND

Many scholars consider Hinduism to be an umbrella, under which shelter diverse religious strains or traditions that have existed in India since prehistoric times. There is no Hindu "church," and orthodoxy is at best a fluid affair. Generally Hindus are held to revere the Vedas, sacred texts going back to the Aryans who invaded India from the northwest perhaps 4000 years ago. As well, Hindus have supported the caste system that has divided Indian society into four main groups and many more subgroups. The main groups have been the priests, the warriors or administrators, the farmers and merchants, and the laborers. A fifth group, the outcastes or untouchables, have been the lowest of the low, given the tasks that the rest of Indian society considered defiling: taking away the sewage, slaughtering animals, and so forth.

The basic concepts justifying the caste structure of Indian society and forming the building blocks of the Indian worldview have included karma, dharma, yoga, and moksha. Karma is the moral law of cause and effect. In Indian thought, a person has become what he or she presently is through the actions of numerous previous lives. Karma therefore is linked to the idea of reincarnation. Nature is a pool of bodies (matter) vivified by various souls. People pass from death to rebirth, so painfully that escaping from this passage is the goal of the loftiest Hindu religious teaching and striving. Karma determines whether one is progressing or regressing in one's goal of escape. If one acts virtuously, one will make progress. If one acts viciously, one will fall back. Yet how one acts, and what character one has, are both shaped by one's previous behavior. Hence, Hindu thought about the destiny of the self can appear contradictory. On the one hand, there is the obligation to act well (a responsibility that presupposes freedom of choice). On the other hand, there is the great pressure of one's karma, accrued from previous lives, which can approach the force of fate. Still, when Indians have been asked why some people are at the top of the social ladder, living as priests, and others are at the bottom, living as workers or outcastes, their traditional response has been karma: people are born into their castes as a result of their behavior, and so character formation, in previous lives. If workers wish to ascend the social ladder, gaining the better chance for complete escape from the cycle of death and rebirth (*samsara*) afforded priests, they should strive with might and main to fulfill their caste responsibilities and cleanse their souls.

Such caste responsibilities are the gist of dharma. Dharma generally means "teaching," and so somewhat approximates the Jewish understanding of "Torah." But the most practical form of dharma has been the rules, both codified and informal, that have suggested the rights and duties of the priest, the warrior, the trader, and the worker. The three upper castes have been eligible for Hindu ceremonies for the "twice-born," the most important of which has been investiture with a sacred thread looped around the shoulder. The thread signifies the person's commitment to the spiritual task of so purifying the soul or self (*atman*) that he or she would make significant progress toward escape from samsara. The dharma elaborated in the classical Hindu law codes has spoken of the responsibilities of priests to recite the Vedas, of warriors to safeguard the commonweal and maintain order, of farmers and tradespersons to work diligently and give honest measure. Virtually all of the dharma has been directed toward men, since the Hindu understanding of female humanity has begun with the assumption that being born a female is a result of bad karma. Thus to gain escape from samsara women would have to be reborn as men. The main responsibilities of Hindu women have been to serve their husbands docilely and be fertile, above all by producing male children.

Yoga denotes discipline, so the various yogas that Hinduism has sponsored have been so many disciplinary ways of improving one's karma and advancing toward escape from samsara. Some of the yogas have targeted the body, trying to increase its composure, suppleness, and docility to the mind and will. The classical yoga of Patanjali sought complete freedom from both bodily and mental restraints. As the yogi advanced along the path to such freedom, he or she became more passive, less engaged with action and thought. At a level of consciousness deeper than sleep, where one's awareness had no specification, one would verge upon what Mircea Eliade has called "enstasis": complete self-possession. Nothing in the world, one's imagination, one's mind, or one's will would dictate or even greatly influence one's pure, self-possessed spirit. Free of all the desires, the needs, the graspings that karma depends upon to keep people trapped in samsara, one might become a truly free spirit and so escape the sufferings of conditioned (unfree) existence.

This escape or release is moksha. When pursued by the intellectual yogas that sought understanding, moksha could be seen as the fruit of enlightenment. Having finally grasped the true nature of reality, one could no longer be trapped by desire, karma, or samsara. For many intellectual yogis the true nature of existence spotlighted the presence of the absolute, often called Brahman, as the actual reality of all existent things. The Vedanta school of philosophy founded by Shankara (788–820 C.E.) was the most rigorous in speaking about Brahman. For Shankara, only Brahman truly, ultimately exists. Any perception of the independent existence of creatures, limited beings, is an illusion. So moksha is the death of illusion as well as the death of enslaving desire. The yogas that dealt with purifying action or work taught that one could escape karma and desire by acting without concern about the results of one's actions (not caring about success or failure, only about right intention). The yogas that dealt with emotion, especially with ardent love of a manifestation of divinity such as the god Krishna, taught that if one loved purely, seeking the absolute under the guise of a winsome god, one could escape samsara and gain union with the absolute. Moksha therefore had both negative and positive connotations.

Described by negation, it was the end of craving, illusion, and death. Described positively, it was a state of being, awareness, and bliss, and so a participation in the deathless truth of Brahman.[1]

The Vedic literature that Hindus have venerated as their Scripture possessed the seeds of this core complex of ideas. At the end of the Vedas, in the Upanishads, one finds a strong instinct that the key to release from suffering and gaining fulfillment lies in joining oneself to the One that must exist behind the multiplicity of physical things. Apparently this poetic philosophy was largely the product of the Aryan culture that gained ascendancy in northern India during the second millennium B.C.E. The native Indian tradition, as expressed in the archeological remains of such pre-Aryan sites as Harappa and Mohenjo-Daro, well-developed cities, probably possessed an orderly ritual focused on purification and a great interest in natural fertility. Some scholars consider "Hinduism" the amalgamation of the Aryan and native traditions into a sprawling complex of various gods, goddesses, ideas, and rituals. Orthodoxy, in the sense of tidy doctrinal formulas, has never been the Hindu interest. Often Hindus have advanced their theology by straining for a conjunction of opposites. To express the ineffable, transcendent character of ultimate reality, they have sanctioned a great range of different myths, symbols, ideas, and religious practices. Thus divinity often has been represented as androgynous, and also as encompassing both the power of death and the power of life. Some Hindu sects have focused on sexuality as the locus or best symbolic expression of the life force, not hesitating to depict divine couples copulating. Other sects have urged an extreme asceticism, to the point that members have gone completely naked.

If we consider the first syntheses of Aryan and native ideas to have been mature by about 600 B.C.E., and to mark the first, foundational phase of Hindu history, we can demarcate a second phase, running from about 600 B.C.E. to about 300 C.E., as dominated by challenges to these first syntheses. Most notably the Mahavira (the founder of Jainism) and the Buddha arose to challenge the dominance of the priestly caste that had gained control over Vedic ritualism and to propose reforms that would make religion more personal and interior. These reformers were joined by many Upanishadic thinkers. Together they laid the foundations for Hindu idealism: conviction that the mental or spiritual aspects of the human being and external reality are the things one must control, if one is to gain enlightenment and moksha.

From about 300 to 1200 C.E. Hinduism went through considerable reform and elaboration, appropriating the insights of those who had challenged it, expanding its law codes and devotional literature, and unleashing powerful theisms centered on gods such as Krishna and Shiva that had great success among the unlettered masses.

From about 1200 to 1947 large parts of India were subject to foreign rule, first that of Muslims come from the West and then that of British traders. Hinduism remained the basic worldview or cultural system of the Indian majority, but millions converted to Islam. The British influence was more to Westernize Indian law, education, government, and military matters than to convert Indians to Christianity. In fact many Christian ideas took root among educated Indians, but Hinduism remained the religious expression of Indian culture. Since India gained independence from Britain in 1947, it has suffered partition into Hindu and Muslim portions. Pakistan and Bangladesh were carved from the traditional Indian territories. Within present-day India millions of Muslims, as well as some Jains, Sikhs (followers of a religion that blended Hindu and Muslim ideas), and a few Buddhists complicate the question of a Hindu culture, as do some secular Indians. Nonetheless, because there are more than 600 million Hindus in India alone, Hinduism continues to be a potent factor in world politics.

STORIES

Hinduism produced the world's longest poem, the Mahabharata, which has offered all Indians a treasury of stories about the gods and heroes of the earliest times. Tradition says that the poet and sage Vyasa dictated the Mahabharata to Ganesha, the elephant-headed god who has been revered as the remover of all obstacles, bringer of good fortune, and patron of writers and thieves. Early in the Mahabharata Ganesha tells how he got his strange appearance:

> "I was born fullgrown from the dew of my mother's body. We were alone, and Devi [his mother] told me, 'Guard the door. Let no one enter, because I'm going to take a bath.' Then Shiva [his father], whom I had never seen, came home. I would not let him into his own house. 'Who are you to stop me?' he raged. And I told him, 'No beggars here, so go away!' 'I may be half naked,' he answered, 'but all the world is mine, though I care not for it.' 'Then go drag about your world, but not Parvati's [his mother's] mountain home! I am Shiva's son and guard the door for her with my life!' 'Well,' he said, 'you are a great liar. Do you think I don't know my own sons?' 'Foolishness!' I said. 'I was only born today, but I know a rag picker when I see one. Now get on your way.' He fixed his eyes on me and very calmly asked, 'Will you let me in?' 'Ask no more!' I replied. 'Then I shall not,' he replied, and with a sharp glance he cut off my head and threw it far away, beyond the Himalayas. Devi ran out, crying, 'You'll never amount to anything! You've killed our son!' She bent over my body and wept. 'What good are you for a husband? You wander away and leave me home to do all the work. Because you wander around dreaming all the time, we have to live in poverty with hardly enough to eat.' The Lord of All the Worlds pacified her; looking around, the first head he saw happened to be an elephant's, and he set it on my shoulders and restored me to life. 'Parvati was happy again, and that is how I first met my father,' said Ganesha, 'long, long ago.' "[2]

The story illustrates the domestication of the gods that Hinduism accomplished. While Shiva and the other deities could appear in awesome, fear-inspiring guises, they had a homey side. Most of the major gods were paired in marriage. Here we catch a glimpse of how popular Indian culture thought about the marriage between Shiva and Parvati. Stereotypic is the notion that women do the physical work and men do the dreaming: poetry, philosophy, yogic pursuit of enlightenment and liberation. Shiva traditionally has been cast as the erotic ascetic. On the one hand he has been associated with the sexual energy necessary for life and creativity. On the other hand he has been associated with the strivings of those seeking release from the world of birth and death. In the Hindu trinity (Brahma, Vishnu, Shiva), Shiva is the destroyer—the one who brings the death and dissolution out of which a new phase of the endless cosmic process emerges.

Despite all his lofty titles, the Shiva of this story is a feckless husband, always wandering off. When he does come home, he injures the child dearest to his wife's heart, out of ignorance about activities occurring in his household. The argument between Ganesha and Shiva represents archetypal tensions between sons and fathers, just as the spat between Parvati and Shiva represents archetypal tensions between women and men. Hindu mythology allowed traditional Indian culture to project many of its fears, angers, and hopes onto a large screen. Contemplating their problems blown up to heroic portions in the lives of the gods, Indians were better able to cope with them. The gods to whom the average Hindu has prayed usually have had defects or pains that have made them approachable. The comic appearance of Ganesha, with his elephant's head, big belly, and robust appetite made him especially popular. Hindu prayer therefore could be quite familiar. For every need and season, there has been a divine figure, maternal or lordly, to whom to turn.

The Bhagavad-Gita, Hinduism's most popular religious classic, occurs in the midst of the Mahabharata. The Gita ostensibly tells the tale of a great war between the leading families of prehistoric times, but most of its chapters discourse on secrets of the spiritual life. At the outset of the Gita, Arjuna, a young warrior, discusses with Krishna, who has taken the guise of an attendant, his sadness at the prospect of war. The only result will be relatives killing one another—carnage and madness. Krishna gives Arjuna a twofold response. First, he explains that each caste must fulfill its designated responsibilities, which for warriors include fighting. Second, he explains that the gist of the human being, its core self, is spiritual and so cannot be touched by the sword. On this frame, the Gita weaves back and forth between elaborations of the potential of the human spirit to gain union with divinity and release from samsara and elaborations of the responsibilities necessary to maintain the social order.

Much of the Gita's teaching is yogic, explaining how one may quiet the senses and move below the imagination and reason to rest at the foundations of the self, where its kinship with the pure divine spirit is apparent. Krishna also speaks about how to purify one's action, so that it is not defiling, and how to deal with divinity through love. The revelation that comes in the last chapter of the Gita, where Krishna discloses that he loves those who revere him, fueled the devotional theism that has dominated popular Indian religion since the era of reform and elaboration that began around 300 C.E.

Two selections from the last chapter of the Gita should convey its eclectic character and wealth as a source of religious inspiration. The first selection expresses mainstream yogic convictions:

"Man is qualified for reaching the Divine when his meditation is pure and properly directed, when he controls himself steadily, when he has done away with sound and other nourishment of the senses, cast off desire and aversion, learned to observe solitude, eat moderately, control speech, body, and mind; when he is always intent on the practice of meditation, devoted to equanimity, no longer centered in his ego, freed from reliance on force; from pride, desire, anger, attachment to possessions; when he is unselfish, at peace. Having reached the Divine, and perfectly peaceful, he knows no sadness and has no cravings. Equal-minded to all creatures, he reaches the supreme devotion to me."[3]

The second selection expresses the bond that bhakti, emotional religious love, can establish between Krishna and the devotee:

"Listen again to my supreme word, to the highest of mysteries. I truly love you. Therefore I shall tell you what is best for you. Turn your mind to me, devoted to me. Doing your rituals for me, bow to me. You will come to me. I promise it to you surely. I love you. Passing beyond appearances, come for refuge to me alone. I shall set you free from evil. Do not be anxious. You must never tell this to a man who is devoid of religious zeal, of love, or to one who cannot listen to instruction, or to one who shows indignation. Whoever in supreme love and worship for me makes this highest mystery known among my worshipers shall certainly come to me. No one renders me service more precious than this man's, nor will there ever be anyone whom I love more on earth."[4]

The cult of Krishna in fact drew many bhaktas convinced that ardent love of the god was their best hope for fulfillment. Some of the most popular stories about Krishna concern his relations with the gopis—girls who herded cows. Krishna was portrayed as a handsome youth winning the gopis over, ravishing them in love, and then leaving them. The gopis would weep and lament the loss of their lover, symbolizing the pains of the religious spirit bereft of God. In this way erotic love became a figure for the mystical pursuit of union with gods such as Krishna. Many religious festivals celebrated the stories about Krishna and Shiva that gave the common people hope of salvation, and many devotional practices arose to help people express their love.

An example of the imagery typical of ardent followers of Krishna occurs in the following selection of Bengali religious literature. Bengal is an area noted for its intense religious festivals. The flute is Krishna's special symbol, calling his followers to dalliance with him: "How can I describe his relentless flute, which pulls virtuous women from their homes and drags them by their hair to Shyam as thirst and hunger pull the doe to the snare? Chaste ladies forget their lords, wise men forget their wisdom, and clinging vines shake loose from their trees, hearing that music. Then how shall a simple dairymaid withstand its call?"[5]

For the allegorists, every human soul was like a simple dairymaid, helpless when the beauty of Krishna came calling. The destiny of those who tried to accept the god's overtures of love and pursue union with him was to suffer the searings of passion.

Leaving worldly things behind, such people could become lost in their quest for divinity, which on occasion would succeed enough to justify all their troubles.

PRAYERS

We have mentioned investiture with the sacred thread, the ceremony by which members of the three upper castes entered upon their status as "twice-born" capable of reaching enlightenment and moksha. From that ceremony many Hindus carried away a life-long love of the *Gayatri,* a verse from the Rig-Veda (3:62:10). A. L. Basham has described the significance of the child's formal exposure to the Gayatri: "The ceremony also involved the whispering of the *Gayatri* in the ear of the initiate by the officiating brahman [priest]. This is a verse from a hymn of the *Rg Veda,* addressed to the old solar God Savitr, which is still looked on as the most holy passage of that most holy scripture. It is repeated in all religious rites and ceremonies, and has a position in Hinduism rather like that of the Lord's Prayer in Christianity, except that the Gayatri may only be uttered by the three higher classes. . . . 'Let us think on the lovely splendour of the god Savitr, that he may inspire our minds.' "6

The traditional view of the Vedas considers them a collection of utterances from inspired seers. They represent how reality appeared to those whom the gods moved to see it rightly. The Vedas therefore convey what Hindus have considered revealed truth. Interestingly, such revealed truth has aimed at the mind more than the heart. Hindus have not denied the importance of the heart, but their predilection has been to rectify the misaligned mind, to clarify the darkened intellect. The great obstacles to enlightenment and liberation (moksha) have been desire and ignorance. Desire has rooted in ignorance: if one saw rightly one would not grasp at impermanent pleasures. The scriptures and gurus therefore have aimed at correcting the mind. If one could dispel ignorance, both individual fulfillment and social order would follow.

Thus it is characteristic that the Gayatri, perhaps the most familiar and best loved Hindu prayer, should be a call to think or ponder or contemplate. What ought one to think upon? The splendor—light, brilliance, beauty—of Savitr, an ancient solar deity. Like the Greeks and the other foremost representatives of Indo-European culture, the Indians correlated mind and sky. The light of day supplied by the sun was like the light of understanding. Both Indians and Europeans provided chthonic (underworld) deities to correlate the earth and the human subconsciousness, but pride of place went to heaven and mind. To make spiritual progress was to ascend—to go up toward the heavens, raising one's vision and ideals so that they better matched those of the gods dwelling on high. Indeed, this directive to contemplate Savitr expresses the Indian conviction that the mind would become like, if not identical to, what it contemplated. If one attended to Savitr, one would become clearer in mind and sunnier in disposition. If one made the splendor of Savitr a great treasure, one would live an elevated life, lofty with wisdom and virtue.

In the liturgy for the dead, the prayers dealing with the heavenly destiny one hoped for the deceased reenforced the equation of heaven with light. Thus Rig Veda 9:113:6–11 speaks of how the intoxicating ritual drink, Soma, might take the worshipers to the realm of Indra, heavenly god of the storm, whose dwelling place is replete with light:

"Where the priest, reciting the metrical words and handling the pressing stone, exults in Soma, through Soma creating, O Purifier, bliss, glow, Soma-juice, for Indra's sake! Where light unfailing ever shines, where dwells the Sun, in that deathless world, place me, O Purifier, beyond harm's reach. Flow, Soma-juice, for Indra's sake! Where the Son of Vivasvat holds sway, the shrine of heaven where the waters flow ever young and fresh, there make me immortal. Flow, Soma-juice, for Indra's sake! Where Men move at will, in the threefold sphere, in the third heaven of heavens, where are realms full of light, in that radiant world make me immortal. Flow, Soma-juice, for Indra's sake! In the place of vows and eager longings, the realms of the golden Sun, of libations and fullness of joy, there make me immortal. Flow, Soma-juice, for Indra's sake! Where happiness and joy abound, pleasures and delights, where all desires find their fulfillment, make me immortal. Flow, Soma-juice, for Indra's sake!"[7]

The correlation of an intoxicant with visions of heaven may raise disturbing questions, but we should remember that Soma was a ritual drink whose effects usually were confined by the ceremonies of which it was part. If it freed the imagination to travel beyond ordinary perceptions and thoughts, that travel was supposed to be in search of gods who would purify the imagination. The correlation of heavenly light with immortality is another noteworthy feature. Hinduism has tended to think of the human spirit as essentially pure. If freed of the mire of ignorance and desire, the human spirit would show itself naturally apt for light and life. No principle of incarnation on the Christian model has stood up for the rights of matter, arguing that matter must have something congenial to divinity if divinity chose to make matter the mode of its personal presence and self-revelation. Certainly Hinduism has numerous rituals that utilize matter, as well as gods (avatars) who give divinity a human appearance. But the Hindu instinct, like the Platonic, has been that matter entraps the human spirit and must be subdued if not eliminated. The knotted dialectic one finds in biblical religion, where matter and spirit are intrinsically related and share a common falling away from God in sin, has no strict parallel in Hinduism. Moral failure, corruption, or disease certainly is admitted, but the body bears more of the responsibility than the spirit, the core self.

For the saints who took bhakti to the heights of union with God, a holistic sense of the self, often expressed in imagery of the heart, helped to combat dualistic tendencies to separate body and spirit. Still, a saint such as Kabir (1440–1518) could conceive of a loving union with God as an entry into a universal spirit. This universal divine spirit both gave reality its basis and transcended barriers between different religious traditions. Thinking this way made Kabir something of a religious revolutionary:

"His was a religion which derived its life from what was best among both the Hindus and the Mohammedans. However, he disliked the bigotry and superstitions of all formal religions and was consequently persecuted by both the Hindus and the Mohammedans. With him and his followers, such as Ruidas and Dadu, we find a religion which shook off all the traditional limitations of formal religions, with their belief in revealed books and their acceptance of mythological stories, and of dogmas and creeds that often obscure the purity of the religious light and contact with God. Kabir considered the practice of yoga, alms, and fasting, and the feeding of Brahmins [priests], not only useless but improper without the repetition of God's name and love for Him. He discarded the Hindu ideas regarding purity, external ablutions and contact with so-called impure things with as much force as he rejected the Mohammedan belief in circumcision or the requirement that a Brahmin should wear a holy thread, or any other marks of caste."[8]

When it came to his prayers, Kabir was consistent and sought a God beyond the partialities of any particular tradition:

"When I turned my thoughts toward God, I restrained my mind and my senses, and my attention became lovingly fixed on Him. O Bairagi [a disciple], search for Him who neither cometh nor goeth, who neither dieth nor is. My soul turning away from sin, is absorbed in the universal soul. . . . If God dwell only in the mosque, to whom belongeth the rest of the country? They who are called Hindus say that God dwelleth in an idol: I see not the truth in either sect. O God, whether Allah or Ram [a Hindu divine name], I live by Thy name. O Lord, show kindness unto me . . . with both mine eyes I look, but I behold nothing save God; mine eyes gaze affectionately on Him."[9]

The prayers of a mystic such as Kabir understandably deal more with praise of God and desire for union with God than with petitions for help. Kabir wants God to take him from sin and darkness, to draw him into the divine embrace and light. He knows that his need for help goes to the roots of his being, where his finitude seems to separate him from his beloved. But Kabir has little concern with obtaining a better job, better prospects for his children, relief from an arthritic hip, rain for the fields, and the other simple, pragmatic projects of daily life that dominate the petitionary prayers of most traditional peoples. For Hindus, taught by popular religion to venerate the gods at household shrines and make them protectors against misfortune, much prayer has been for material benefits. The great poverty of the subcontinent has assured that the gods would be a source of relief and otherworldly assistance. Psychologically, if not physically, Hindu petitionary prayer has provided a safety valve. What the material world did not supply the gods might. Objective analysts often call this sort of prayer "superstitious." If by that term one means that reason has been subordinated to irrational hopes, no doubt much petitionary prayer is superstitious. For the average Hindu, illiterate and impoverished, the spiritual world has been alive with forces, evil and good, that one had to avert or enlist. The gods gave a happier face to this world, so often one went to the gods like a child asking a parent to clear the closet of ghosts. Popular Hindu prayer and rituals have insisted that the gods make a difference in daily life, especially by healing sick bodies and spirits. Granted the actual circumstances of many Hindus, such an insistence can seem to cross the border of superstition and enter the realm of praiseworthy faith.

RITUALS

To the outsider, Hinduism can seem to entail a host of religious rituals. Ceremonies for the life-cycle, the seasons of nature, and festivals of particular gods and goddesses keep up a constant stream of excitement. Consider, for example, the possibilities for ceremonializing the very first phases of the life-cycle:

"Of the various samskaras, or personal ceremonies, in the life of the pious Hindu the first three took place before birth: these were *garbhadhana,* to promote conception, *pumsavana,* to procure a male child, and *simantonnayana,* to ensure the safety of the child in the womb. The birth ceremony (*jatakarma*) took place before the cutting of the umbilical cord, and involved the whispering of sacred spells (*mantra*) in the baby's ear, placing a mixture of honey and ghee [clarified butter] in his mouth, and giving him a name, to be kept secret by his parents until his initiation [with the sacred thread]. At birth the child and his parents were ritually impure, and therefore not entitled to take part in ordinary religious ceremonies until some ten days later, when the child was given his public name and the period of impurity ceased. Minor rites of infancy, not always looked on as particularly sacred, were the ear-piercing ceremony, and the *niskramana,* when the child was taken out of the house and shown the sun for the first time.

"More important was the first feeding (*annaprasana*). In the child's sixth month he was given a mouthful of meat, fish, or rice (in later times usually the latter) mixed with curds, honey and ghee, to the accompaniment of Vedic verses and oblations of ghee poured on the fire. The tonsure (*cudakarma*) took place in the third year, and was confined to boys; with various rites the child's scalp was shaved, leaving only a topknot, which, in the case of a pious brahman, would never be cut throughout his life. Another ceremony, not looked on as of the first importance, was carried out when the child first began to learn the alphabet.

"Many of these ceremonies are now rarely if ever practiced in their full form, and it is doubtful if every ancient Indian family, even of the higher classes, performed them regularly, especially in the case of girls. Their number, however, shows the importance of the child in the life of his parents."[10]

The child was important in the life of its parents, as well as in its own right, because the Hindu conception of the life-cycle provided for steady progress toward better karma and enlightenment. The first of the four major stages in the classical schema for the life-cycle had the child apprenticed to a master for study of the Vedas. At the end of such study, the child was expected to marry and enter gainful employment. In the third stage, when they had seen their children's children, Hindus were to detach themselves from the world and enter upon a contemplation that would join their study of tradition with what they had learned through experience. Those who felt they had become enlightened about this combination might, in a fourth phase, wander freely, begging their food and instructing others by word and example about the primacy of God, life's real treasure.

In what one might call folk Hinduism, a plethora of rituals focusing on either the family shrine or pilgrimage sites fills the typical villager's year. Thus one anthropologist studying villagers of the Himalayas noted the presence of many shamanic ceremonies, in which the typical pattern was for the shaman to bring before the group concerned the god or spirit thought responsible for a sickness or misfortune. The basic idea was that the god or spirit had taken offense at some illicit behavior, or some neglect of religious devotion, and so caused the trouble. The puja or family prayer focused on the household shrine may also seek relief from particular troubles, but its more constant goal is a reverence for the family's gods that will keep them helpful.

Concerning pilgrimages to noteworthy shrines, the most popular ceremonies involve either simple ways for pilgrims to express their need for healing, better fortune, and other personal wishes or celebrations of the festival of the god or goddess to whom the shrine is dedicated. In the case of Himalayan Hindus, pilgrimages to local shrines seem also to have brought caste impurity into play, because frequently priests and other upper-caste Hindus resented the presence of pilgrims from lower castes:

"Pilgrimages are frequently undertaken for reasons similar to those motivating worship of village or household gods. A person suffers from some trouble or disease such as, in one recent case, weeping ulcers. A shaman is consulted and advises the sufferer to worship at a particular holy place, in this case Kedarnath. The person vows to do so and sacrifices a goat to his god, whereupon he recovers. At the first opportunity he undertakes the journey to fulfill the vow. People also go merely to see the temple or to give charity there in order to attain credit toward the next life. A number of middle-aged high-caste men of Sirkanda [the village the anthropologist was studying] have been on pilgrimages to Hardwar, Dedarnath, Badrinath, and a few to distant Gaya. At least one woman and one low-caste man have been to Badrinath. Many tales of the wonders of these holy places and the miracles which regularly occur at them are current in the village as a result of reports brought back by pilgrims or traveling ascetics and priests. The fewer villagers who have seen a place, the more numerous and amazing are the stories. Many villagers — about twenty-five men — have been to Hardwar to bathe in the Ganges or attend funeral rites, and there is relatively little lore about it, but there are many stories of the wonders of remote Kedarnath.

"Equally current, among low-caste people, are the stories of discrimination, disappointment, and denial of access to these places experienced by their caste-fellows who have made the trip, despite official denial of such practices. The one village blacksmith who had gone to Kedarnath nonplussed the priest by his presence (fellow pilgrims had complained) and was not allowed access to the temple. Eventually he was shown the temple padlock and told to worship that."[11]

One sees, then, that in ritualistic situations caste becomes a matter of purity or fitness to enter the formal presence of the gods. The Hindu instinct about such matters is quite physical. It is one's bodily being (considered shaded, for example, by the recent birth of a child, menstruation, or existence in a low caste) that is in question. One need not have sinned or done anything offensive spiritually. (Yet inevitably physical impurity carries moral overtones, because of the unity of the psychosomatic personality.) Inasmuch as much Hindu ritual concerns righting physico-emotional relationships ("vibrations," one might say) between the petitioner and the deity, caste is considered significant.

The ancient background for Hindu ritualism is significant. In the Vedas one finds indications that the priests considered their sacrifices necessary for the maintenance of the cosmos. The words and actions of the Vedic rituals moved the forces responsible for the functioning of both natural and human affairs. Thus at the foundations of Hinduism the entire existence of human beings was ritualistic—a matter of constant interaction with the gods. Thomas Hopkins has described the fire sacrifice central to the early priestly synthesis of Vedic religion and then generalized about its implications for human beings' place in the cosmos:

> "There could be no higher claim for ritual power than is made in the *Satapatha Brahmana,* that the fire sacrifice is identical with the universe, and that the creation and maintenance of the universe depend upon the continued performance of the sacrificial ritual. The lasting contribution of the Brahmanas [treatises elaborating the priestly view of reality] was the development of a comprehensive theory and a consistent world view to support this claim. The effectiveness of mantras, the magical potency of ritual actions and speech, and the creative power of tapas [devotional heat] all were comprehended within the Brahmanical system.
>
> "The structure of this system was an elaborate set of identities and correspondences binding together the cosmos, the sacrifice, and man. The sacrificial ritual was the central and unifying factor in this system. It provided both the conceptual tools by which man could understand the universe and the practical means by which he could control it. Those who had access to the 'triple science,' to *brahman* [ultimate reality], knew where they stood in relation to the cosmos and knew what had to be done to make their life and afterlife successful."[12]

When the priests' synthesis broke down, because reformers such as the Mahavira and the Buddha claimed persuasively that the rituals had become formalistic and did not deliver an experiential enlightenment or liberation, this view of the cosmos receded into the background. Nonetheless, it appears to have influenced the Hindu sense of ritual up to the present day. When celebrating a festival of Shiva, Krishna, or one of the many forms of the Great Mother Goddess (Mahadevi), for example, the pious worshiper feels engaged with the powers that shape the physical world. Shiva is the Lord of the Dance that keeps the world going and finally winds down into episodic destruction. Krishna is a manifestation of Vishnu, the divine force that preserves the world in existence, giving all things their goodness. The Mother Goddess can be kindly and soothing, but she can also represent the force of death with which birth seems aligned. In such forms as the fierce Kali, bedecked with a garland of skulls and her tongue lolling to lap up human blood, she can be a terror to mortal human beings, warning them to become serious about their souls. Ritual therefore has been the staff of Hindu life and prayer. In their many ceremonies, Hindus have shown an acute sensitivity to the omnipresence of divinity and to the constant human need to beg help and offer worship.

CHRISTIAN REFLECTIONS

Perhaps what first strikes the Christian trying to appreciate Hindu prayer is the abundance of imagination and desire to contact the divine. Virtually every aspect of existence has appeared in Hindu ritual as a presence or modality of the divine. If the yogi has believed that an imageless trance is most conducive to realization of ultimate reality, the ardent bhakta has stood up for the rights of love. If the average villager worshiped a local divinity and feared noxious spirits, the average priest thought that traditional ceremonies could exorcize such spirits and bring people into harmony with the will of the gods. Hindu mythology yields to none in its exuberance for stories about the divine exemplars. Hindu philosophy has few peers when it comes to mapping the makeup and potential of the human spirit. The Hindu instinct thus has been radically catholic: anything may mediate divinity, because everything depends on divinity for its being and significance.

Does this mean that Hindu prayer has suffered from confusion about the transcendence of God, not realizing that the true God has to exceed all forms, material, imaginative, and even spiritual (inasmuch as the human spirit is only analogous to the divine spirit)? Probably not, but perhaps so. The Hindu philosophers knew of the negative way toward divinity. In the Upanishads one finds sages teaching that Brahman is "not this, not that." Indeed, those reflecting on the nature of Brahman sometimes spoke of a hidden or unmanifest divinity—a depth or transcendence that assured that ultimate reality would always be impenetrable to limited human minds. Nonetheless, one finds more desire in Hinduism to merge the human spirit with the divine than one finds in Christianity—more tolerance of pantheism. For some of the Upanishads the human spirit (atman) ultimately is one with Brahman, in such wise that appearances of distinction or separation must be called illusions. In fact, those most strongly persuaded of the presence of divinity in the being of all realities frequently came to consider the entire realm of human experience illusory (maya). They did not mean that a fifty-pound bag of sugar wouldn't break a yogi's toe. They meant that, in final perspective, nothing finite exists independently of God and so one can say that only God finally is.

There are analogies to this position in Christian philosophy, of course, where the aseity (independent existence) of God has been a central attribute. But Christian prayer has been steered away from pantheistic forms of mysticism by several central Christian doctrines. The Christian doctrine of creation so stressed the independence of God and gratuity of God's making the universe that Christians were not likely to identify God with anything created. The Christian doctrine of sin strengthened this instinct, making human beings well aware that they were as far from God morally as ontologically. Finally, the Christian doctrine of the incarnation admitted the complete union of divinity and humanity in the case of Jesus, but it also taught that these two natures remained distinct, and that the union achieved in the case of Jesus was unique—not something any other human being could achieve.

This means that the Hindu view of the divine-human relationship (and consequently of prayer) closest to mainstream Christianity has been that of the theologians of love, such as Ramanuja, who placed whatever unity could occur between divinity and humanity in the bond of affection established by divine grace. This bond did not annihilate the difference in being between divinity and humanity, but it did accomplish a dedication of the saintly lover to God so intense that psychologically only one will and desire remained.

Christians might learn much from the confidence with which the typical Hindu has approached prayer, whether ritualistic or informal. Though the Hindu gods have frightening, judgmental aspects, their overall appearance is welcoming. Not only does their multiplicity symbolize the divine desire to appeal to every station and type of personality, but their iconography reenforces this message. The many arms of a god such as Shiva suggest his power to control all forces, his resources for helping all petitioners. Even the androgyny of some of the iconography of Shiva, like the statuary that depicts divine consorts coupling sexually, has encouraged the notion that divinity is familiar with and composed of everything essential to human existence, everything that human beings know bodily and spiritually.

One might question whether the Hindu doctrine of karma and rebirth more aids or dilutes Hindu prayer, but a sympathetic reading of karma and rebirth is instructive. Because the Hindu life-cycle is not limited to one try at gaining virtue, maturity, and enlightenment, Hindus have found counsel to be patient with both divinity and themselves. The Western anxiety about a definitive judgment at death that would send one to an eternal hell or heaven has its analogues in popular Hinduism, where heavens and hells are also important, but the Hindu sense that time is vast and circular probably has blunted some of the narcissism that anxiety about judgment can carry. The line between a fatalistic acceptance of the karmic situation and a profoundly religious surrender to divine providence sometimes seems slight. Inasmuch as Hinduism has encouraged people to do their best and not worry excesssively about the outcome, it has nurtured a praiseworthy trust in God.

Christian prayer has not been burdened with a consciousness of caste like that of Hindu prayer. Christians have not had to feel ashamed of their social station or line of work, though of course many have (because the psycho-social dynamics responsible for caste have operated in Christian hearts and groups as well as Hindu). Numerous Hindu thinkers found religious reasons for undercutting caste and relegating it to the world of illusion that enlightenment cast aside, but the Hindu mainstream did not achieve the democratic instinct expressed in such New Testament landmarks as Galatians 3:28, where Paul makes baptism a great social leveler.

Princes or poets, Hindus or Christians, all people seeking a generous, positive yield from the comparison of Hindu and Christian instincts about prayer might take to heart the conviction that God is the sole fulfiller of the human heart. Both the Hindu and the Christian saints chant this conviction night and day. And so both relativize all the achievements that we tend to turn into defenses against God's exhaustive claims. Neither will let us think that our power or wealth or even virtue can substitute for naked communion with God. To be sure, death teaches this lesson across all cultures and traditions, but both Hindu and Christian saints have found it at prayer. When God has touched their souls, they have realized that nothing else is a worthy treasure. Everything else is a potential idol, virulent unless we place it in the context of the priority of God.

It may seem strange to credit Hinduism with so monotheistic an instinct, granted the multiplicity of divinities in Hinduism and the charge that many Hindus have worshiped stones, trees, and genitalia. On reflection, it is not strange. Considered generously, with the benefit of the doubt we would want others to grant us, the Hindu use of multiple images for God, and the Hindu sanction of considering creative human energy divine, can be called sacramental. Through their rituals, Hindus have been expressing their confidence that the creative power responsible for the world has designed human beings so that their use of material forms for worship is inevitable. Most of those bowing at a shrine of Krishna have not confused its particular imagery with divinity in itself, any more than most of those praying at a shrine of the Blessed Virgin have confused her with the ineffable God. In both cases people have groped their way toward the One they hoped would heal them of their heartsickness and justify their lives.

How much difference the Hindu stress on ignorance, in contrast to the Christian stress on sin, has brought into Hindu prayer is hard to say. There is a point at which ignorance becomes willful, just as there is a point at which willful wrongdoing darkens the understanding. The Hindu saints have begged forgiveness and cleansing, just as the Christian saints have. If Christians have found Jesus the most adequate expression and revelation of all this, only those ignorant of Hindu worship of Krishna or Shiva could fail to note similarities to Christian soteriology (view of salvation) in Hinduism. Hinduism speaks of grace, just as Christianity does. Hinduism does not grant Krishna or the other gods the full historicity that Christianity grants Jesus in making him completely human, but that does not mean that Krishna has not played an enormous role in Hindu culture, and so in Hindu history. One can speak of Krishna mediating salvation to Hindus, letting the word "salvation" mean just what it means in Christian parlance: healing and divine life. When Hindus pray to their gods for help, they enter a process more like than unlike the process Christians enter. In both cases the goal is healing and divine life, even when those praying are not clear that that is what they are ultimately seeking.

Chapter 5

BUDDHISM

BACKGROUND

Buddhism traces its beginnings to Gautama (536–476 B.C.E.), the prince whose insight brought him the title "Buddha" (Enlightened One). According to legend, Gautama's father learned before the child's birth that the son was to become a spiritual hero. The birth was miraculous, the child issuing from his mother's side and nature applauding. Because his father wanted to keep Gautama at home, minding the family kingdom, he tried to ensure that the boy would want for nothing. Every manner of pleasure and satisfaction was provided. Gautama married a lovely maiden and soon was the father of a healthy son. But all was not well. By the time he was in his late twenties the prince was restless. His restlessness clarified one day when he escaped from the palace compound and met a funeral procession. It was the first time he had seen a corpse or been forced to think about death and it shook him. The traditions say that on subsequent forays the prince encountered disease and old age, which added to his spiritual crisis. How could human beings go about their daily affairs apparently disregarding their certain painful fate? Why weren't all people bending might and main to solve the problem of suffering expressed in death, disease, and old age? Soon his restlessness became such that Gautama slipped away from the palace, his wife, and his child, leaving in the dead of night to join battle with the problem of suffering.

His first maneuver was to apprentice himself to some teachers

78

of meditation and asceticism. From them he learned how to quiet his mind and descend to the depths of consciousness. He was so ardent in his asceticism that when he pressed his navel he could feel his backbone. But still the problem of suffering remained, grinning at him confidently. Leaving his teachers, Gautama decided he had to look to his own resources. He finally sat himself under a pipal tree and resolved not to get up until he had conquered suffering. The evil one, Mara, sensing that his power was threatened, sent his beautiful daughters desire, discontent, and distraction to weaken Gautama's effort, but to no avail. Eventually the prince passed beyond the knowledge of the shamans, which encompassed awareness of all his previous lives, and beyond the knowledge of the mystical philosophers, which grasped the connection between beings' actions and their karmic fates. With the thunderclap that signifies gigantic achievement, Gautama became the Enlightened One by breaking through the knot of ignorance and perceiving the solution to the bedrock, definitive human problem of suffering.

The Buddha expressed his enlightenment in terms of the Four Noble Truths: (1) All life is suffering; (2) the cause of suffering is desire; (3) stopping desire will stop suffering; (4) the way to stop desire is to follow the noble eightfold path of right views, right intention, right speech, right action, right livelihood, right effort, right mindfulness, and right concentration. As Buddhists traditionally have understood the noble eightfold path, it has stipulated an interlocking program with three main parts: wisdom, morality, and meditation. Right views, right intention, and right speech stem from grasping how reality actually is constituted. Right action, right livelihood, and right effort stem from a commitment to living morally, in keeping with how reality actually is constituted. Right mindfulness and right concentration are the gist of meditation, where wisdom can become experiential and moral convictions draw nourishment.

The Buddha spent the second half of his life preaching the way of life that his enlightenment had convinced him could bring other people to freedom from suffering. Generally his accent was more therapeutic and practical than speculative. One of his well-known analogies was that human beings are like a man shot with a poisoned arrow. The point is get the arrow out, not to worry about who shot it, what trajectory it traveled, or how strong the bow was. Another famous image painted the whole world as burning with desire and so bound for karmic bondage. The point was to quench the fire of desire, so that neither the eye nor the ear, neither the loins nor the brain, was immersing the individual in the mechanics of pain.

The Buddha clearly drew upon the prevailing Indian beliefs of his time, retaining the notions of karma and rebirth. Even his analysis of the painful human condition in terms of the bondage created by desire was not new. But the times were ripe for reform and renovation, as the somewhat parallel ventures of the founder of Jainism and the writers of the Upanishads showed. The genius of the Buddha was to fashion a radical reinterpretation of Indian tradition that took it to a new depth of religious experience and a new precision of expression. The Buddhists soon broke with mainstream Indian tradition by denying the relation between the individual self (atman) and the foundation of creation (Brahman) assumed by many Indians and canonized in the Upanishads. For the Buddhists there was no self. Selfhood was the deepest illusion. Similarly, there was no ultimate reality distinct from phenomena and stabilizing them. Rather all beings formed an "empty" circle and interacted with one another causally. Buddhists used the traditional term "samsara" to designate this circle and agreed with Hindus that bondage to it kept one in a painful cycle of deaths and rebirths. But as their philosophers and meditation masters appropriated Gautama's intuitions, they came to consider nirvana (release from samsara) a pure and ineffable state of unconditionedness. One could say that nirvana and samsara were one, because everything real in samsara finally depended on the unconditioned (unlimited, and so alone fully real) character of nirvana. But the preferred description of nirvana was that it is what happens when the flame of desire has blown out—something quite positive.

The Buddha had lived a simple life, in the good weather wandering to preach to new crowds and in the rainy season sheltering in the forest. He had begged his food or accepted charity from wealthy disciples, lived in celibacy, and devoted himself to meditation and teaching. The community that gathered around him soon consisted of both laypeople, living in the world and carrying out the responsibilities of family life, and people who wanted to imitate Buddha's celibacy, poverty, and full-time dedication to meditation and teaching. This latter group became the backbone of the Buddhist community (sangha), forming a monastic elite. The Buddha accepted women into his monastic life (reluctantly, some sources say), so from early in Buddhist history nuns have been significant. With the Buddha himself and his teaching, the sangha has constituted the three "jewels" of Buddhist life. Indeed, the ceremony in which one formally becomes a Buddhist amounts to "taking refuge" in the Buddha, the Dharma, and the Sangha.

Buddhism grew quickly during Gautama's lifetime, and it continued to grow after his death, because he had formed a solid band of disciples who themselves had experienced enlightenment on his model. Shortly after his death, Buddhist tradition holds, such disciples held a congress to collect memories of Buddha's teaching and practice, thereby somewhat standardizing Buddhist faith. During the third century B.C.E. the Buddhist emperor Asoka tried to make Buddhist principles the rationale for his statecraft, and throughout the rest of the pre-common era Buddhism waxed and waned as a respected Indian religion (another native sect, in the eyes of many). Various doctrinal and disciplinary disputes led to the rise of a variety of different Buddhist groups, and eventually a general division arose between those who claimed to be keeping pure the old traditions (Theravadins, also known as Hinayanists) and those willing to innovate (Mahayanists). Both groups continued to preach the four noble truths, advocate wisdom, morality, and meditation, and take refuge in the three jewels. But the Mahayanists reached out more to the laity, which led to a proliferation of theistic devotions, myths, and popular rituals. They also sponsored more speculative innovation, developing Buddhist metaphysics and downplaying the historical Gautama in favor of the Buddha who was the intellectual light (Logos or source of intelligibility, a Westerner might say) of the world. Finally, the Mahayanists changed the notion of the Buddhist saintly ideal from the mainly self-concerned model of the Theravadin arhat to the altruistic model of the bodhisattva (Buddha-to-be) who would postpone entry into nirvana in order to labor for the salvation of all living things.

By the end of the first millennium of the common era Buddhism had lost the battle for India's religious affection to Hinduism. Nonetheless, Buddhists were doing well to the east, due to missionary ventures that had found great success at least as early as the first century of the Common Era. Theravada tended to predominate in the lands closest to India—Ceylon (Sri Lanka), Burma, and Thailand, for example. Farther east—in Vietnam, China, Korea, Japan—Mahayana traditions prevailed. Tibet took more from India than from China but developed its own distinctive Buddhism, which some commentators consider a third branch (*Vajrayana*) comparable to Theravada and Mahayana. Today there are over 250 million Buddhists around the world and Buddhism is one of the leading forces in ecumenical discussions among representatives of the world religions. Buddhism has deeply penetrated the cultures of east Asia, often commingling with Confucianism, Taoism, Shinto, and other native traditions. Devout Buddhists celebrate many religious holidays, feel drawn toward meditation, and have available a rich fund of philosophical, ethical, and mystical traditions, as well as gorgeous achievements in the arts.

STORIES

Many of the earliest stories about the Buddha and his leading disciples portray them in dialogue, teaching Buddhist principles through a give-and-take with serious inquirers. One of the most famous such dialogues depicts the sage Nagasena in discussion with the Greek king Menander. The discussion focuses on the Buddhist teaching that there is no self. Menander has questioned this teaching by asking Nagasena what unifies the various bodily parts associated with "Nagasena"—to whom do they belong? Nagasena has denied that his identity resides in any such things, but he has also rejected the King's conclusion that "Nagasena" therefore means nothing.

To explain this rejection and advance his own, Buddhist position, Nagasena then takes the offensive:

"Your Majesty, how did you come here—on foot, or in a vehicle?"

"In a chariot."

"Then tell me what is the chariot? Is the pole the chariot?"

"No, your Reverence."

"Or the axle, wheels, frame, reins, yoke, spokes, or goad?"

"None of these things is the chariot."

"Then all these parts taken together are the chariot?"

"No, your Reverence."

"Then is the chariot something other than the separate parts?"

"No, your Reverence."

"Then for all my asking, your Majesty, I can find no chariot. The chariot is a mere sound. What then is the chariot? Surely what your Majesty has said is false! There is no chariot! ..."

When he had spoken the five hundred Greeks cried, "Well done!" and said to the King, "Now, your Majesty, get out of that dilemma if you can!"

"What I have said was not false," replied the King. "It's on account of all these various components, the pole, axle, wheels, and so on, that the vehicle is called a chariot. It's just a generally understood term, a practical designation."

"Well said, your Majesty! You know what the word 'chariot' means! And it's just the same with me. It's on account of the various components of my being that I'm known by the generally understood term, the practical designation Nagasena."[1]

The story illustrates the philosophical turn that Buddhist teaching often has taken. Although the Buddha thought that speculation had limited use, the culture of his time forced him to express himself to serious inquirers in terms of their philosophical interests, all the more so when he was claiming that there is no such thing as a self separate from its human parts or attributes.

This doctrine of no-self did not reject the commonsensical

attribution of identity to people such as Nagasena. But it did make the point that Nagasena was the collection of his parts and not some esoteric entity underlying them. Thus "selfhood" could be held lightly and the desires that kept tying the self to objects in the samsaric world could be undercut. If one began to think of oneself as a collection of elements in flux and joined by relations of mutual influence, one probably would become "lighter." One's fingers could be pried from the attachments that kept one bound to the karmic cycle of deaths and rebirths and so in great pain. Nagasena was trying to get King Menander to shift his view of both himself and the world. Such a shift, fully executed, would have amounted to enlightenment, coming in the mode of Buddhist wisdom.

A contemporary story, told by the American Zen master Philip Kapleau about his own experience of enlightenment, captures the experiential and meditational side of this key Buddhist goal. Kapleau had gone to Japan in the mid-1950s, disgusted with his life. Slowly he had become more and more involved with Zen Buddhism, eventually making pursuit of enlightenment through its disciplines his full-time occupation. After more than three years of practicing meditation and attending various intense meditational retreats, he finally got the experience he had been seeking:

"Hawklike, the roshi [master] scrutinized me as I entered his room, walked toward him, prostrated myself, and sat before him with my mind alert and exhilarated.

" 'The universe is One,' he began, each word tearing into my mind like a bullet. 'The moon of Truth—' All at once the roshi, the room, every single thing disappeared in a dazzling stream of illumination and I felt myself bathed in a delicious, unspeakable delight. For a fleeting eternity I was alone—I alone was. Then the roshi swam into view. Our eyes met and flowed into each other, and we burst out laughing.

" 'I have it! I know! There is nothing, absolutely nothing. I am everything and everything is nothing!' I exclaimed more to myself than to the roshi, and got up and walked out. . . . I feel free as a fish swimming in an ocean of cool, clear water after being stuck in a tank of glue, and so grateful. Grateful for everything that has happened to me, grateful to everyone who has encouraged and sustained me in spite of my immature personality and stubborn nature. But mostly I am grateful for my human body, for the privilege as a human being to know this Joy, like no other."[2]

Kapleau's experience of enlightenment was typical in coming as the climax of intense meditational effort. Some Zen schools teach that enlightenment can just as well come easily, emerging as the natural evolution of faithful practice, but the Rinzai practice in which Kapleau was schooled has stressed laborious effort. As his description indicates, enlightenment brought Kapleau great joy. He felt at one with everything in existence and freed of all the restrictions that had been chaining his being to pain. His predominant emotion was joy, and his mind had become holistic. No longer did he stress the dichotomies and differences among things. No longer was his first instinct to stress his distinctness from the rest of reality. With enlightenment came the sense that he was alone, that he was everything, and that nothing was. What predominated was simple being, in such a fashion that no particular beings ultimately existed. And his insight was its own warrant. Because his experience was so intense, he could not doubt it for a second. Such confidence is what Zen masters look for when they scrutinize their disciples. The signs of enlightenment show in the person's entire bearing even more than in the answers the person's mind brings forth.

For Zen Buddhism, which comes in the line of Mahayana schools and stresses meditation, enlightenment incarnates the wisdom passed down from the Buddha and grounds the morality expected of Buddhists. Such traditional precepts of Buddhist ethics as the prohibitions against murder, lying, theft, unchastity, and taking intoxicants seem obvious, when one has experienced the truth of the Teaching. Similarly, much in Japanese culture and other cultures shaped by Buddhism derives its mystique from what we might call the natural mysticism that is the goal of Buddhist meditation. Floral arrangement, the tea ceremony, archery, gardening, the martial arts, and recently methods of business management all have been touched by Zen discipline geared to produce enlightenment and finally justified by enlightenment.

For lay Buddhists, not inclined to assault enlightenment by might and main, the goal that often prevails is improving one's karma, so that one's next lifetime might place one in better circumstances for reaching nirvana. Such Buddhists may also pray quite devotionally, asking the Buddha and the Bodhisattvas for help with family troubles, work, sickness, and the like. Kuan-yin, the motherly Bodhisattva who has served much of East Asia as a kindly goddess, exemplifies the allure in much popular Buddhism. Visiting a shrine to her in a park in central Tokyo in 1976, we authors saw dozens of snapshots of babies whose parents credited their birth to the kindly intercession of Kuan-yin (whom the Japanese call Kannon). Each snapshot represented a story of pain, petition, faith, and success. No doubt countless other stories, many of them less happy, moved in the wind around the shrine, but the positive stories prevailed. So we were reminded that Buddhism has served its practitioners on many different levels, as a comprehensive and successful religion must.

What one might call folk religion, close to the earth and the seasons, has loved the Buddhist festivals and rituals for warding off misfortune. The practical and ritualistic Buddhism of groups such as Nichiren Buddhists, who chant scriptural verses in the expectation of improving their this-worldly fortune, represents one way that Buddhist doctrine has been cast. The stress on faith in Amida, the Buddha who rules over the Western Paradise, characteristic of the followers of Shinran, a much-loved Japanese Buddhist master who left monastic life to marry because he wanted to draw closer to the common people, represents another influential way. The stories of enlightenment in Zen monasteries are more dramatic, but for estimating the totality of Buddhist prayer the tokens left in shrines to Kuan-yin may be equally important.

Analysts who treat Buddhism as a nontheistic or even atheistic religion have to make several important distinctions, if their analyses are to square with actual Buddhist practice. If one considers divine the figure to whom people pour out their deepest hopes and needs, then Kuan-yin and numerous other foci of Buddhist devotion have been gods and Buddhism has been theistic. If one considers the joy and gratitude that enlightened Buddhists such as Kapleau have experienced as a mark of otherworldly grace, then Buddhist experience raises the question of to whom, or to what ultimate reality, such joy and gratitude refer.

PRAYERS

Devotional Buddhism, somewhat in contrast to meditational Buddhism, tends to use vocal formulas to petition help. For example, the anthropologist Melford Spiro, studying lay Burmese (Theravadin) Buddhism, noted the use of classical lists of desirable Buddhist virtues in healing rites. Such lists may be found in the sutras (discourses) attributed to Gautama. Reciting them has become part of a holistic effort to cure psychosomatic pain: "When treating a patient, Burmese native doctors recite the Virtues as well as prescribing medicine in order to cure him. Or, in an entirely different domain, prisoners (both criminal and political) may recite this spell as a way of obtaining their release. Often it is recited while saying the [Buddhist] rosary."[3]

One grouping of the virtues distributes them among the three jewels of Buddhist faith:

"Virtues of the Buddha: 'the Exalted One, Arahant, supremely enlightened, proficient in knowledge and in conduct, the Blessed One, who understands the world, peerless tamer and driver of the hearts of men, the Master, the Buddha for gods and men, Exalted one.' Virtues of the *Dhamma*: 'Well proclaimed by the Exalted One is the Norm, relating to the present, immediate in its results, inviting all, giving guidance, appealing to each, to be understood by them that can understand.' Virtues of the *Sangha*: 'Well practised is the Exalted One's Order of Disciples, practised in integrity, in intellectual methods, in right lines of action — to wit the four pairs, the eight groups of persons — this is the Exalted One's Order of Disciples, worthy of offerings, oblations, gifts, salutations, the world's peerless field for merit.' "[4]

This mantric use of traditional formulas to obtain help deserves comment. First, we should note the long religious tradition of attributing a magical efficacy to consecrated words. In the case of originally Indian religions such as Buddhism, such a tradition goes back to Vedic times, when the effectiveness of the sacrifices of the brahmins was thought to depend on an exact recitation of appropriate formulas. Second, we should note the fuller power that words have in oral (nonliterate) cultures or folk traditions not much shaped by books. Third, the point in the Burmese recitations of the virtues seems to be that by calling to mind the admirable attributes of the Buddha, the Dharma, and the Sangha one activates them positively. To the mind convinced of karmic influences, such an activation amounts to stimulating a helpful moral causality—getting good karma rolling. Fourth, individual Burmese Buddhists may also use such formulas to express deeper feelings of trust, hope, or even worship. For analysts who think that the crux of prayer is what goes on below the words and thoughts, in the person's heart, even mantric formulas are capable of expressing the love of the divine mystery in which authentic religion finally reposes.

It is interesting that the typical Buddhist ceremony for either a holy day or the formal meditational session of a group usually includes the recitation of portions of the Buddhist scriptures. The canon of Buddhist scriptures (Tripitaka) is immensely long, so the selections can vary considerably, but the instinct to chant some words attributed to the Buddha or sanctioned by long usage as fitting expressions of Buddhist attitudes shapes the majority of Buddhist rituals. Thus even Zen Buddhists, whose theory may downplay any special divinity of Gautama and stress the buddhanature of each living being, often will use flowers, incense, pictures, and scriptural chants to enrich their meditations. Similarly, Buddhists adhering to Tibetan traditions often use mantras and mandalas (sacred shapes) to enrich their meditations. Indeed, some Tibetan schools emphasize an imaginative identification with divine figures—bodhisattvas—reminiscent of the Christian practice called "the application of the senses." The theory behind such imaginative practices differs from Christian theory, yet those familiar with the longstanding Christian defense of ikons as sacred presences will find some similarities. The Tibetan Buddhists tend to think that one is activating divine potentialities in the human composite, yet sometimes the divinities that are the focus of the practices are so vivid that they seem more objective—independent of the human psyche—than subjective. All the more so is this the case in folk or lay Tibetan Buddhist rituals, where a goddess such as Tara usually is approached with the sort of trust and hope extended by East Asian Buddhists to Kuan-yin.

For example, a long prayer to Tara known as "The 108 Names of the Holy Tara" includes the following laudatory verses:

"Goddess of the perfection of wisdom, Holy Tara who delights the heart, Friend of the drum, perfect Queen of sacred lore who speaks kindly, with a face like the moon, shining brilliantly, unconquered, with a yellow garment, the great Maya, quite white, most strong and heroic, greatly formidable, capable of fierce anger, slayer of evil beings, quite calm, calm to behold, victorious, blazing with splendour. . . . These 108 names have been proclaimed for your [the believer's] welfare; they are mysterious, wonderful, secret, hard to get even by the Gods; they bring luck and good fortune, destroy all sin, heal all sickness, and bring ease to all living beings. When one recites them three times, intelligently, clean from having taken a bath, and with concentration—then before long one attains to the splendours of royalty."[5]

The number 108 seems arbitrary: the devout worshiper of Tara could go on endlessly. One image leads to another, making a garland of consecrated pictures and phrases. The person using a prayer such as this wants practical help, yet something more contemplative also is at work. A certain delight in picturing the features of the Goddess and thereby dwelling in her presence is the real key. The petitioner finds it good to be with the Goddess through the imagery traditional for her. She is an ikon, an imaginable presence, of the ultimate holiness and goodness to which the petitioner's heart goes out. She is a form for the "wisdom that has gone beyond" — the light of enlightenment that disperses the shadows of ignorance and so uproots the sources of pain.

Although this imaginative sort of prayer has been very important in devotional Buddhism of all branches (Theravadin, Mahayana, and Tibetan), the yogic beginnings of Buddhist spirituality have ensured that an imageless religious practice also would be important. Thus both Theravadin and Mahayana meditation masters have urged the use of images only as helps to concentration. Ideally meditators would focus on nothing particular, letting go of both pictures and ideas, preparing the mind for the enlightenment that images best trigger when the spirit is collected and unattached.[6]

The Zen use of koans — enigmatic sayings calculated to tease the mind away from dichotomies and toward enlightenment — illustrates this thesis. The point to having a disciple bore into a saying such as "the sound of one hand clapping," or "your face before your parents were born," is to tie the mind so that attention will not squirm away. As well, it is to insinuate that the true nature of reality escapes the either/or mentality of the unenlightened. Enlightenment consists in an experience that expresses the personality as a whole. Equally, it is an experience that finds reality itself to be whole.

What, then, is the disciple such as Kapleau doing when he or she bellows a koan such as "mu" ("not" — one of most popular koans) night and day? Much depends on the interpretational framework the person trying to answer such a question employs. From a Zen perspective, the person is stirring up the "buddhanature" (enlightenment being) innate in all living creatures. Also at work, for those willing to add theses from devotional Buddhism, is the influence of the compassionate Buddha, who is "skillful in means to save" all creatures from their pain. One could interpret Kapleau's experience as a reception of grace, on Buddhist as well as Christian grounds, grace meaning in Buddhist terms feeling the goodness of reality and so verifying what Gautama revealed.

For the person who follows a saint such as Shinran, such grace is the paramount feature of the Buddha. Life in the world is so difficult that Amida Buddha has greatly simplified the conditions of salvation. If one merely calls upon the name of the Buddha with faith, one can break out of the karmic cycle and hope for escape to the Western Paradise, where Amida dwells. This Western Paradise is the Buddhist equivalent of the Christian heaven or the Muslim Garden—a realm of complete fulfillment. Less devotional Buddhist sects downplay the imagery of jewels and flowers that proliferates in devotional speculations about the Western Paradise. For them the final goal of all meditation or prayer, as of all wisdom or morality, is nirvana—escape from karma, rebirth, and suffering. By being the negation of such negatives, nirvana is wholly positive. It is a state of freedom from all the constraints, internal and external, that press upon most creatures and give them pain. To desire such freedom one must put aside ordinary desires and become the master rather than the slave of one's passions and mind. Whether through devotions, ascetical practices, studies, or meditational exercises, one must become converted to a new, enlightened way of perceiving the world and feeling about it. This is probably the major goal of mainstream Buddhist prayer, even though we should not underestimate tendencies toward worship of Buddhist divinity.

RITUALS

The Buddha himself taught that rituals were of no avail—in fact, that they could be hindrances to religious progress. In teaching this, he was commenting adversely on the Hindu ritualism of his day. Just as he found the Hindu gods ineffectual, so he found chanting the Vedas and performing the various Hindu sacrifices ineffectual: they did not bring people to enlightenment and so to the experience of release from samsara.

Nonetheless, by the beginning of the Common Era Buddhists had developed a series of ceremonies to commemorate key moments in the life of the Buddha, and they had sanctioned the use of images of the Buddha for devotion. Believers were counseled to concentrate on the Buddha being imaged, rather than on the wood or stone or metal of the statue, but such images gained status as holy objects. Concerning the events of the Buddha's life that became occasions for celebration, three have

stood out: the day of the Buddha's birth, the day of his enlightenment, and the day of his death (his entrance into nirvana). In
Theravadin countries the tendency has been to combine the
observance of these three events into a single celebration, called
Wesak, which occurs in May. Mahayana countries separate the
celebrations. The pilgrim Fa-hsien reported seeing celebrations
of the birth of the Buddha in India early in the fifth century
C.E. The rituals he observed were part of the monastic regime
and occurred on the eighth day of the fourth lunar month. Later
the Buddha's birthday was celebrated at the imperial court in
both China and Japan. Nowadays both monks and laity celebrate
it on April 8:

> "The central altar is a flower-bedecked shrine, especially
> made for the occasion, with a figure of the infant Sakya-
> muni [Buddha] standing in a basin of sweet tea. The
> shrine, covered with spring flowers, symbolizes the garden
> of Lumbini, where the Buddha was born. The standing
> figure with one hand pointing to the heavens and the other
> to the earth depicts the legend surrounding the Buddha's
> birth, in which he is said to have taken seven steps to the
> east and proclaimed to the world, 'Heavens above, heavens
> below, I alone am the World-Honored One.' At that time,
> the legend continues, the earth shook, beautiful music re-
> sounded throughout the universe, and flower petals and
> sweet tea rained from the sky. Following the procession of
> monks or priests and the chanting of sutras, the believers,
> both young and old, bow in obeisance to the Buddha im-
> age, pour sweet tea over it with a ladle, and receive flowers
> and sip sweet tea."[7]

The observance of the Buddha's enlightenment, held on De-
cember 8, is more solemn. The ceremony recalls the Buddha's
renunciation of both hedonism and extreme asceticism, as well
as his forty-nine days of meditation under the Bodhi (Knowledge) Tree. Zen Buddhists tend to hold intensive meditational
retreats around this time, trying to capitalize on the good aura
surrounding the memory of the Buddha's great triumph. During such retreats monks may rise as early as 2:00 A.M. and

devote as much of the day as they can to meditation.

Observances of the death of the Buddha traditionally were celebrated on the fifteenth day of the second lunar month. Rituals were in place in India by the seventh century C.E. In China sixth-century emperors led ceremonies. Today the ceremony tends to be observed on the 15th of either February or March. Prominent in most ceremonies is a large representation of the scene of the Buddha's deathbed. Traditionally, the Buddha lies on his right side, in peace, surrounded by his disciples, animals, and birds. Some monasteries reenact the cremation of the Buddha's body and repeat his last sermon.

A ceremony especially developed for the laity and sometimes considered the most important of the Buddhist ritual year focuses on redemption from hell. Legend has it that the layman Moggallana had a vision of his mother suffering in hell. To save her, he performed the charitable act (recommended by the Buddha) of feeding hundreds of monks. By this charity he was able to gain his mother's release from hell. Moggallana became a model of the filial piety especially prized in East Asia. Today the recollection of his action, called Ullambana, functions as an occasion to remember the dead and honor one's ancestors. People prepare their household shrines to receive the spirits of the dead, visit the family grave to clean it, and adorn the family grave with new flowers. Some groups light bonfires to guide the spirits of the departed back home for the celebration. This ritual owes as much to pre-Buddhist convictions about spirits as to Buddhist views of the afterlife, but its association with dances, singing, lanterns, and drumming has made it very popular.

In East Asia Buddhist monks became the principal celebrants of funeral rites, in good measure because Buddhism became revered as having a more profound philosophy of death than Confucianism, Taoism, or Shinto. The *Tibetan Book of the Dead* describes in great detail the 49 days after death, during which the person's spirit may still gain merit, enlightenment, and nirvana. Death is considered the breakup of the "heaps" that compose the selfless human entity. The person has the option of adhering to karmic attachments, and so being fated to enter another circuit of the samsaric process, or breaking free. Tibetan Buddhism therefore developed a manual for helping the deceased make one last great effort. Popular Buddhist funeral rites have honored the good works of the deceased and have included prayers that he or she would have a fortunate afterlife.

Buddhists also have ritualized such matters as "giving" (dana), through which they have expressed support of the monastic order or compassion for other living beings. Such compassion, following the example of the Buddha himself, has been a hallmark of the Bodhisattvas and so represents something for all Buddhists to imitate. Along with adhering to the basic ethical precepts and practicing meditation, giving has constituted the triple cord of Buddhist piety. One of the classical sutras supporting giving says,

"Whoever, moral in habit, gives to the poor in moral habit a gift rightfully acquired, the mind well inspired, firmly believing in the rich fruit of kamma [karma] — this is an offering purified by the giver. Whoever, poor in moral habit, gives to those of moral habit a gift unrightfully acquired, the mind not inspired, not believing in the rich fruit of kamma — this is an offering purified by the recipient. Whoever, poor in moral habit, gives to the poor in moral habit a gift unrightfully acquired, the mind not inspired, not believing in the rich fruit of kamma — this is an offering purified by neither. Whoever, moral in habit, gives to those of moral habit a gift rightfully acquired, the mind well inspired, firmly believing in the rich fruit of kamma — I assert this gift to be of abundant fruit. Whoever, without attachment, gives to those without attachments a gift rightfully acquired, the mind well inspired, firmly believing in the rich fruit of kamma — I assert this gift to be a gift abundant in gain."[8]

The repetitions and formulaic character of the text suggest that it was to be memorized. The stress on intention is typical of Buddhist counsel about action in general and ceremonial action in particular. As long as the thing given, or the deed done, itself is pure, the great issue is the intention with which one acts. For the Dhammapada, perhaps the best-loved portion of the Tripitaka, a person finally becomes what the person thinks. Indeed, the karma that a person produces is a direct function of the thoughts, good or evil, that the person thinks. Many Buddhist rituals therefore became principally occasions to act out pure intentions. In fact, in monastic settings all the regular events of the day have become rituals, because each is an occasion for consecrating actions (work, meditation, recreation, sleep) by pure intention. Unlike the Western analogues to pure intention, the goal is not to offer each action to God, as a sacrifice. Rather it is to do the thing as it ought to be done, seeing and reverencing it rightly. The underlying conviction, strongest in Mahayana schools, is often that each creature is intrinsically pure—a presence of buddhahood.

Buddhist monks have also ritualized confession of their faults, following the counsel of canonical texts attributed to Gautama. One of the customs of Hindu ascetics of the Buddha's day was to hold a period of fast twice each month. The Buddha accepted this custom into the routine of his Sangha and the period of fast became an occasion for monks to confess their faults and receive forgiveness. Buddhist monastic legislation expanded to cover a great variety of faults that might be confessed. Some (murder, adultery) were considered reason for expulsion from the order. Others were considered lesser faults meriting lesser punishments. Once again, the understanding of confession and forgiveness has differed from Western analogues. The Buddhist concern has been to reverse the bad karma the offenses have generated, while the Western concern has been to offer repentance and reparation to a divinity personally offended by sin.

Buddhists have developed a wealth of other rituals, some for the home and some for local temples, in which they have celebrated the events of the agricultural year or reverenced the burial places of venerable saints. The general pattern at popular temple festivals has been to allow the faithful to venerate an appropriate statue of the Buddha or Bodhisattva, hear or recite scriptural passages, and offer flowers and incense.

CHRISTIAN REFLECTIONS

Buddhist meditation and prayer place a premium on awareness and refinement of consciousness. While Buddhists make a

place for petition and faith, the strongholds of monastic practice
and theory stress a purification of consciousness that might di-
lute desire to the point where it would evanesce. Concommi-
tantly, those engaged in Buddhist meditation usually are seeking
enlightenment, either in the dramatic experience of having one's
awareness flip over and show the world to be one and pure —
exactly as the masters have proclaimed it to be — or in the more
sedate experience of expressing one's beliefs about the enlightened nature of all reality by simply sitting and being oneself.
The celibacy practiced by Buddhist monks and nuns has extended a deep-seated Indian instinct that emotion, desire, and
their bodily foundations are the great impediments to wisdom
and nirvana. On the whole, this has not meant despising the
body or developing a dualism in which matter and spirit became
antagonistic. Rather it has meant trying to make the whole body-
spirit composite both dispassionate and energetic. By disciplin-
ing body, mind, and will, Buddhist ascetics have tried to remove
impediments to nirvana, and ties to karma. The schools that
accepted the dialectics of philosophers such as Nagarjuna, which
equated nirvana and samsara, had special grounds for making
the goal of their disciplines this-worldly vigor, beauty, power,
and effectiveness. The success with which one could paint, fight,
conduct business, and the like was a good sign of the efficacy of
one's discipline. Much energy, good health, and wisdom in the
guise of detached objectivity have flowed from both Theravada
and Mahayana practices.

The special emphasis given the imagination in Tibetan practices underscores how the imagination can mediate between the
body and the spirit, the will and the emotions. The Tibetans
have been conscious of what Westerners call libidinal energies,
realizing the power of such energies either to bind people to
samsara or propel them toward enlightenment. Thus one reads
stories of leading Tibetan masters who counseled violating such
social taboos as eating meat or drinking alcoholic beverages. The
point was not to become the slave of one's good ethical precepts.
Ethical precepts are not an end in themselves. If one cannot see
how they serve in the order of means, they can be entrapments.

The desire to enlist libidinal energies and avoid legalistic en-
trapment has been prominent in the Indian tantric tradition on

which Tibetan Buddhism has drawn. Both Hindus and Buddhists have practiced tantric rituals, the most notorious of which have involved illicit sexual union, either imagined or actual. In the full-blown practices, ritualists would often consider themselves divinities whose union of male and female forces went to the foundations of the order of the natural world. Hindu iconography stressed this ritual sexual union or yoga (*maithuna*) more than Buddhist, but the same basic practices have appeared in Buddhist tantra, especially that called "left hand."

For Christians, the most relevant point seems to be the Buddhist desire to marshal all of the human instincts and faculties into the service of enlightenment and nirvana. While many lay Buddhists have been content to seek a better karmic condition, the most ardent followers of Gautama have taken his experience of complete enlightenment as something they themselves might replicate, however feebly. The Christian parallel would be the view that in his humanity Christ was a forerunner of all who experienced the grace of God to be not only saving but also divinizing. In other words, what God did in signal, unique degree in the incarnation of the Word, God has done in lesser measure for the saints, great and small, who have opened themselves to the divine love. The Johannine writings of the New Testament speak eloquently of believers' sharing in the divine life, like branches participating in the life of the vine. They specify the sharing in the communion of Father, Son, and Spirit to which faith gives access. So, somewhat like Buddhists coming into the treasures of the buddhanature through enlightenment, the Christian mystics have experienced that God's holy love is the substance of their truest being.

Many might accept this interpretation of the Johannine theology and the experience of the Christian mystics and yet consider it to carry little practical significance. If one compares the Buddhist and Christian integrations of theory (wisdom, doctrine) and practice (ethics, meditation), frequently the Buddhist syntheses seem stronger. Much of the reason seems to be the Buddhist stress on meditation as the place where wisdom becomes experiential and ethics gets its power. Certainly Christians have spilt much ink extolling the benefits of prayer, but seldom does Christian prayer emerge as the place where the primary doctrines of Christian faith (Trinity, Grace, Incarnation) may be experienced and the basic law of Christian ethics (love of God and love of neighbor as self) may be empowered. The history of Christian theology shows lamentable eras during which doctrinal and moral theology had little connection with ascetical and mystical theology. Perhaps dialogue with serious Buddhists could solidify the growing Christian conviction that we cannot allow such separations in the future.

When one considers Christian prayer in the light of Buddhist holism, the traditional theses and formulas can be deepened significantly. The Buddhist stress on what people are, in their depths and best potential, can summon forth a parallel Christian stress on what God has given people to be. For Christian faith, interpreting the depths of the creature's potential as communion with God, the light so much praised by Buddhists becomes the twin of the love so much praised by Christ. Light and love go together, as do truth and goodness. The Christian "atmosphere" seems warmer than the Buddhist, because the Christian view of love does not stress detachment (the quenching of desire) as strongly as the Buddhist. As well, the Christian view of love, shaped by the historical fate of Jesus, makes suffering a mystery closely associated with the mystery of evil. The irrationality of sin—evil freely chosen—frustrates the light one associates with God and holiness. The sufferings of Christ on the cross, which have no close parallel in the life of the Buddha, make the tasks of love more knotted and ugly than Buddhist instincts tend to make them. The exemplar of Christian faith, and so both the model and the focus of much Christian prayer, is a man despised, rejected, accounted a criminal, bloodied, and crucified. Christian prayer can never wander far from this scandal. It must always reckon with the revelations about love that the Crucified carries.

Among these revelations may be a useful qualification about the self-purifications that both Buddhist and Christian ascetics and contemplatives tend to desire. If sin is what the Crucified suggests, it goes to the marrow of human freedom and qualifies simple theses about the buddhanature latent in all creatures or the divinization worked by opening human freedom to light and love. Neither of these theses should be rejected, but both should be further scrutinized, lest they fail to reckon with the gratuity of salvation as well as creation.

The gratuity of creation, its having sprung from nothingness, is a solid tenet of Christian faith and a major warrant for the eucharistic character attaching to liturgical prayer. Everything has come down from the Father of lights. But the patterns organizing "everything" generate such conflicts as earthquakes, evolutionary extinction, and cancers. Moreover, the patterns organizing human history show gross and wanton sin, the consequence of which, generation after generation, has been both immense suffering and many obstacles to believing in the goodness of the Creator.

Enter the mystery, facts, and doctrines associated with salvation. Where creation seems relatively amenable to understanding, though of course only clarified and intuited to be an immeasurable mercy of God in light of the history of Christ, salvation seems less penetrable, more murky. What can make human beings whole, and how does one develop the political theses necessary to deal realistically with human beings who are not whole, even though God has offered them ways of becoming whole?

These questions color Christian prayer in whatever hues one associates with humility, struggle, confession of sin, and naked prayer for divine aid. They suggest that the key dispositions are those that keep people going, hoping, trying. It is fine to find purity of heart and intention, a tidy consciousness shaped by a tidy regime. But perhaps it is a greater mercy of God to find that even when our hearts condemn us, God is greater than our hearts. Perhaps the greatest lesson Christ on the cross bears those who would persist in prayer is the assurance that nothing can separate them from God's love, not even their guilt for having contributed to the crucifixion of God's nearest and dearest.

So while Christians should thank God for the manifest wisdom and goodness that divine grace has produced through Buddhist channels, they should also strive to appreciate the blessings of passion and desire entailed by accepting a fully incarnate, suffering savior. The world as it is—torn, as well as beautiful; dirtied, as well as sacramental—enters the divine embrace. God mends the rents, takes away the dirt, and wipes every tear from the eyes of those who cling to Christ, because the love that makes our light has taken our flesh and absorbed all its evil.

Chapter 6

NATIVE AMERICAN RELIGIONS

BACKGROUND

The deepest roots of Native American religious traditions apparently lie in east Asia. Anthropologists now conjecture that the people we call the natives of all the Americas—North, Central, and South—migrated across a land bridge at what is now the Bering Strait. Such migrations probably date to about 10,000 years ago. The people who emigrated would have been hunters and gatherers whose cultures were shaped by the land they inhabited and the game they pursued. They would have been shamanic, in the sense of being attuned to ecstasies that seemed to give them unusually valuable knowledge of the forces ruling their destinies.

Over a considerable period of time, the immigrants filled the entire expanse of the Americas, diversifying their cultures and religious systems as their relations with their given locales evolved. In the far north, those we now call Eskimos (they tend to call themselves Inuit) developed the endurance and skills necessary to survive great cold. The animals key to their survival, such as the seals and elk, figured prominently in their rituals. The Inuit also reverenced the bear and respected the wolf. Eventually their religion laid great emphasis on the ensoulment of all reality. The tragedy of human existence, in Inuit eyes, was that living things have to take life from other living things if they are to survive. Such a taking of life necessitated rituals to placate the souls of the beings killed or offended. It also made people alert to the presence of the spirits of the dead, which might be carrying grudges.

In the eastern woodlands of North America, hunting and gathering predominated until perhaps 3000 years ago. The general economy had people hunting deer, gathering plants, fishing in rivers, and harvesting shellfish along the coasts. In the southwest the game tended to be rabbits while the gathering tended to focus on wild seeds and roots. The Dorset culture of the eastern Arctic that paleontologists date to about 600 B.C.E. produced houses of driftwood or stone and subterranean dwellings with roofs of sod. The Dorset developed stone lamps that burned oil taken from seals and built such ingenious boats as the kayak. By 1200 B.C.E. the culture of the Mississippi Valley featured significant earthen mounds for burial, while in the Ohio Valley around 1000 B.C.E. farmers were growing gourds and squash.

These few indications of the adaptations that the immigrants made on North American soil are enough to suggest the variety in their cultures and so in their religious beliefs. For traditional peoples, oral or literate, religion was the pulse of general culture and could not be divorced from it. To walk the land or navigate the water was to travel in territory overseen and controlled by spirits. The plants and animals with whom human beings had to interact were fellow citizens of a single cosmos. Native Americans certainly distinguished between themselves and the animals who had no speech or apparent rationality, but not so sharply as modern human beings have. Their tendency was rather to ascribe the hunting skill of the wolf or the building skill of the nesting bird to an intelligence analogous to their own. In their visions, the shamans who supplied much of the spiritual leadership spoke with birds or animals, receiving through their ministration crucial information about the future, or the people's standing with their gods, or other matters of moment. Shamanic healers depended on the spiritual powers of plants and animals to rally the strength of the sick. When they went into trance to guide the souls of the departed to the land of happy rest, Native American shamans expected to meet both helpful and potentially harmful spirits along the way, many of which they saw in animal form.

One of the first items to note in the background of Native American religions therefore is the intimacy with nature that thousands of years of living directly from the land induced. Native American traditions often distinguish a Great Spirit who presides over the natural world, and they have many accounts of how the natural world arose from the creative action of such a Spirit or the Spirit's helpers. But such beliefs did not lead to depreciating the natural world or considering it merely raw material for human beings to use as they saw fit. The Native American divinities tended to move through the natural world. Their power and will could be expressed at any striking rock, tree, or stream. The storm could carry their messages, as could the calm or the song of birds. Each of the directions of the compass said something about their presence. The great task of human beings was to walk in harmony with such holy forces shaping the natural world.

The rituals that the different tribes developed tended to initiate members more and more deeply into the significance of such a walk or way of life. Most tribes ritualized birth, coming of age, marriage, and death. They had ceremonies for curing people of various ills and ceremonies for cleansing people of guilt. Contact with the dead, with blood, and with people who had killed animals or other human beings demanded cleansing. Some tribes built sweat lodges to purify the entire psychosomatic personality. Other tribes used solitude to prepare people for visions that could give them direction or reset them on the right path. In general male and female powers were considered both complementary and antagonistic. As complementary they suggested the division of labor many tribes honored: women doing most of the cooking, clothes-making, and caring for children; men doing most of the hunting, warfare, and perhaps farming. As antagonistic they suggested the need to segregate women at times of menstruation and childbirth, when their power to bear forth life was fullest. Similarly, men who had exercised their power to kill, through hunting or warfare, generally required seclusion and purification.

The tribes also developed rich mythologies to explain their

origin, how the world had come into being, and whence their distinctive traditions had derived. Elders of the tribe were the usual repository of such lore, responsible for passing on the traditional wisdom. Elders, often of both sexes, also provided the counsel on which the tribe most depended for its important decisions. The words of elders, shamans, or any people concerned about serious matters or ritual affairs had a resonance hard for people formed by books to appreciate. The immediacy of oral cultures, the direct contact with nature and spiritual forces that tends to prevail, makes such cultures intrinsically poetic. The shaman regularly sings the prescribed rites for healing, because the words are holistic, coming from the heart and wrapping themselves around all the participants. Symbolism is the staff of life in Native American and other oral religious traditions, because all important speech involves naming things that one encounters as pregnant with possibilities, significances, mysteries. The world is vibrantly alive, with forces that can work evil as well as forces that can work good. Anything primordial — the sun, the moon, the blood, the bone — is venerable, soliciting wonder and appreciation. Dreams can be great channels of revelation, and one does not distinguish sharply between what goes on in dreams and what goes on in waking life. Similarly, the distinctions that literate modern cultures have introduced between imagination and judgment, experimentation and deductive theory, all postdate Native American traditions.

These general descriptions also hold for the tribal religions that thrived in Central and South America. Migration from north to south apparently proceeded quite quickly, so that by 9000 B.C.E. or so big game hunters had worked their way through Central America. By 3000 B.C.E. potters were working at villages just south of the equator, and by 2500 B.C.E. people were farming (beans, squash, and potatoes) in the highlands of the Andes.

The great civilizations of the Native Americans developed in Central and South America, where the Olmecs, Mayans, Incas, and Aztecs created impressive cities, social structures, buildings, and religious hierarchies. Among the Aztecs a priestly class presided over complicated sacrifices (some of them human), while warriors dominated a system of slaves. The religious cultures that the Spanish conquistadores encountered in Central America early in the sixteenth century C.E. were the heirs of perhaps 2000 years of history.

For all the peoples "native" to the Americas (all the originally Asian prehistoric migrants) prayer was a natural part of culture. Individuals petitioned the spirits familiar to them from personal visions or tribal ceremonies. Groups reverenced the forces sung in their traditional chants, described in their traditional stories. Most of the great tribal celebrations were religious in the sense of situating the people in terms of their traditional understanding of how the world had arisen and what was required of them to live well in it. Each need for healing or reconciliation drew people back to their central focus: living harmoniously with the awesome powers guiding their destinies, the spirits presiding over life and death. If one was to work well, hunt well, enjoy good health, have healthy and obedient children—that is, to prosper in any way—one had to be on good terms with the spirits, the forces that made things grow, kept away evil influences, and gave peace to the human heart. Those wanting special intercourse with such spirits usually would try to purify themselves, through solitude, fasting, and other ways of sharpening their minds and attuning their hearts. Music and dance could be great allies. But the key thing was to raise one's mind and open one's heart in gratitude and love for the wonder of being a creature privileged to enjoy the beauty of creation and the wonder of life. The coming of white culture devastated Native American traditions, but in recent years some revivals have occurred—enough to make such terms as "Native American spirituality" relevant to today's dialogues among the world's living religious traditions.

STORIES

The stories that Native American tribes told usually had some adaptability. While the basic accounts of creation or how the tribe's most revered ceremonies arose would be held sacred and invariant, many other stories could shift as changed circumstances warranted. In 1886 Frank Cushing, an ethnographer studying Zuni tribes, participated in a round of storytelling. All the people gathered around would contribute tales, and when his turn came he told the European folk-tale of the cock and the mouse. The mouse asked the cock to help him collect some nuts from a tree. The mouse climbed the tree and threw down a nut that hit the cock on the head, splitting his skull. The cock had to get water from the fountain to give to the forest, in exchange for wood to give to the baker, in exchange for bread to give to the dog, in exchange for two hairs to give to an old woman, in exchange for rags to bind up his wound.

A year later Cushing returned to the Zuni and participated in another round of storytelling. To his surprise, he heard one of the Zuni offer the story of the cock and the mouse, but much extended and adapted. Not only had the Zuni added details to ground the story in their own culture, but they had also changed the conclusion. When the cock reached the water, the spirit of the water complained that human beings had been neglecting their duties, not offering gifts in return for the bounty of what they drank and used for bathing. Therefore the cock would have to offer several feathers, which the source of the water (the clouds) might accept to appease their discontent. The cock therefore took four plumes and laid them on the four directions of the spring from which he had asked water. This got him the water, and so the wood, the bread, the hairs, and the rags. The Zuni also added the observation that it was through this accident of being hit on the head with a nut that the cock got his red comb, which looks like the wound he originally suffered.[1]

The story falls in the realm of entertainment more than deep mythology, yet the changes the Zuni worked on it suggest their traditional mind-set. For them nothing so precious as water or wood could be handled in a purely economic spirit. One had to deal with the spirit of the water or the forest respectfully, making clear one's gratitude for the benefits it bestowed and offering something in return. The basic "economy" of the world, as the Zuni saw it, included the return of respect, gratitude, and material gifts from the human beneficiaries to the forces of nature on which they depended. When the cock laid feathers from his own plumage at the four cardinal directions, he was sacrificing to honor the holy powers of life on which creatures depend in all planes. The Zuni could not abide the notion that even the reality depicted in a fairy tale would lack such a sensitivity to honor and gratitude.

Working with South American tribal stories and symbolism, Lawrence E. Sullivan has described the metaphysical depth that Native American notions of how the world came into being and presently is constructed have achieved. Each significant element of the people's habitat usually has attached to it a myth explaining how it gained its present appearance and how it fits into the overall sense of the world that the people possess. This overall sense of the world has changed since the advent of whites, but the regular tendency of most tribal peoples has been to absorb elements of white religion into their traditional worldviews rather than to reject the traditional accounts and take up a completely white worldview. For example, concerning the place of water and rivers in typical tribal cultures Sullivan has written:

"For some South American cultures, to cross through the celestial river or to bathe in the central lake of heaven changes one's existence; immersion in heavenly fluid is an initiation, which, like all acculturations, alters the conditions governing the meaning of one's senses. For the Quechua of Qotobamba, for example, immersion in life-giving waters is required to gain full participation in the life of heavenly space. The universe exists in three cosmic realms. The upper world, called Hanaqpacha, can be reached only after life. It is peopled by God, Christ, the Virgin Mary and those of the dead who have been washed in the waters of Baptism. Around its periphery is Limpu (Limbo), the place where unbaptized children's souls reside. Also on the periphery of Hanaqpacha are zones where animal spirits go after death. The Quechua disposition of heavenly space reflects the fact that initiated humans are beings whose life-condition and ultimate destiny are shaped by the manipulation of water. Such control is evident in the symbolism of ritual washings, in irrigation technology, in ritual beverages, and in cooking. Through the symbolic manipulations of ritual and technology, human knowledge affords control over items that originate in and that define the nature of heavenly space. Like the possession of celestial fire and heavenly plants, the human ability to manage life-giving waters stems from the symbolic foundations of human knowledge. Such knowledge, based on the meaning of sacred symbolism, sets human beings apart from animals in the zoning of residential space in heaven."[2]

South American stories, like those of other oral peoples, are the major vehicle for organizing the symbols through which the people create and express their sense of reality. Creating and expressing their sense of reality is the main "business" of their traditional way of life. Certainly they have to hunt and gain food. Certainly they need housing and clothing and medicine. But their main preoccupation is to understand more and more about the world they inhabit, to enrich their wisdom about the human condition. The stories they tell channel an imaginative effort to contact the mysteries they intuit their reality to hold. Because the mysteriousness of existence attaches to every significant item in their experiential inventory, the rivers and streams, as well as the animals and trees, attract a considerable mythology. In the case of the Quechua of Qotobamba, encounters with Christians have provided more grist for the mythological mill. Baptism suggests an even richer potential in streams and other sources of water than what they had traditionally appreciated, so their heaven stretches to admit a celestial river correlated with the key personages of heaven, as Christianity depicts them.

It takes a great labor of the imagination for anthropologists, and their readers, to enter into the mentality of such tribes and experience the organic character of their symbolism. The "logic" of the stories and symbols of traditional peoples is not the logic suggested by empirical investigations, even those so practical as finding plants to cure the worst sicknesses afflicting one's people. The logic of traditional mythopoeia is more like the logic of dreams and other unfettered exercises of the human imagination. The meaning expressed and developed has sources so deep in the psyche that their roots remain out of sight. Above all, sympathetic study of traditional mythologies reminds us of the desire built into human nature to worship a transcendent reality—a beauty and meaning that might fulfill the human heart's longings.

Florinda Donner, an anthropologist working with tribes of Venezuela, penetrated the native South American mentality sufficiently to grasp the sensitivity to natural beauty that shapes major portions of the native worldview. On a walk late in her stay with her tribe, she shared some of the ecstasy that their attunement to the jungle could produce:

"We reached the top of a plateau eroded by winds and rains, a relic from another age. Below, the forest was still asleep under a blanket of fog. A mysterious, pathless world whose vastness one could never guess from the outside. We sat on the ground and silently waited for the sun to rise.

"An overwhelming sense of awe brought me to my feet as the sky in the east glowed red and purple along the horizon. The clouds, obedient to the wind, opened to let the rising disk through. Pink mist rolled over the treetops, touching up shadows with deep blue, spreading green and yellow all over the sky until it changed into a transparent blue.

"I turned to look behind me, to the west, where clouds were changing shape, giving way to the expanding light. To the south, the sky was tinted with fiery streaks and luminous clouds piled up, pushed by the wind . . . I wanted to speak, to cry out loud, but I had no words with which to express my emotions. Looking at Ritimi and Etewa, I knew they understood how deeply I felt. I held out my arms as if to embrace this marvelous border of forest and sky. I felt I was at the edge of time and space. I could hear the vibrations of the light, the whispering of trees, the cries of distant birds carried by the wind."[3]

Certainly Native American life has never been pure ecstasy, in response to the delights of the physical world. Certainly many Native American stories and ceremonies have had to focus on suffering, physical or mental. Yet the "space" opened in the Native American spirit by attention to the vast natural world and meditation on the symbols and stories drawn from the roots of the psyche trying to respond to this world has afforded Native

Americans considerable esthetic delight and mysticism. One cannot separate holiness, being, and beauty, least of all in the worldviews of traditional oral peoples. To pray has been inseparable from meditating on the foundations of existence and blessing the creative powers for the goodness of what they had made.

PRAYERS

In the traditions of the Lakota (Sioux) about the origin and execution of the Sun Dance, as reported to Joseph Epes Brown by Black Elk, one finds the following prayer: "O Grandfather, Father, *Wakan-Tanka,* we are about to fulfill Thy will as You have taught us to do. . . . This we know will be a very sacred way of sending our voices to You; through this, may our people receive wisdom; may it help us to walk the sacred path with all the Powers of the universe! Our prayer will really be the prayer of all things, for all are really one. . . . May the four Powers of the universe help us to do this rite correctly; O Great Spirit, have mercy upon us!"[4]

The Sun Dance is a complex, rich ritual that offers to God the sacrifice of pain produced by dancing under the sun with leather thongs through one's breast—dancing until the thongs pull through and tear one's flesh. It provides a chance for the people to do penance for their offenses, reassert the priority of God (*Wakan-Tanka*) in their lives, and reconsecrate themselves to the paths laid out by their God. Several things about this brief specimen from the many prayers and symbols associated with the Sun Dance merit comment.

First, notice the familiar way the Lakota have addressed their God. Despite all the awe and adoration they have sent heavenward, they have considered their deity to be parental—the first elder in their family line. At other times Native Americans have given divinity a maternal cast, especially when they have focused on the life-giving earth or the source of the game. But here the main referent seems to be the heavens and the sun, which for the majority of traditional peoples have carried masculine connotations.

Second, notice the belief that the rite to be executed was

given to the people in a vision and imposed as a command by the divine will. Regularly the impetus associated with Native American rituals and standard prayers comes from a divine figure. People reaching out to the ultimate powers want to feel that they are doing something sanctioned by those powers. Otherwise, they might be overreaching themselves. At times this desire to channel their prayer into sanctioned tracks led traditional peoples into a maze of rules and customs about how to perform the stipulated rites. In the accounts that Black Elk gives of the major rites of his people, one finds amazing detail about the kinds of elements to be used and the gestures and words to accompany them.

Third, it is typical of this prayer to associate the people with the powers of nature generally, and to invoke such symbols for the totality of nature as the "four powers" of the directions of the compass. This prayer, as most of those formalized by the Lakota, rose to God on smoke from a sacred pipe. The pipe symbolized the permission God had given human beings to commune with divinity and stood for the spiritual ascent of the people's desires toward God. When it served to reconcile members of the tribe, its human effects drew on the deeper significance the pipe carried as an assurance that humanity and divinity were reconciled enough to allow regular communication: prayers ascending from the earth and visionary wisdom descending from heaven.

The Papago Indians of southern Arizona have long sung songs as their basic way of dealing with both divinity and the other powerful forces at work in their world. For example, when it came time to plant their corn, the men would assemble and "sing up the corn," convinced that without their songs it might not grow healthily. Their songs were modes of power, through which they could work on the world and mold it to their desires. Here is part of the song they would sing to make the corn rise up:

"Evening is falling. Pleasantly will reverberate our songs. The corn comes up; it comes up green; here upon our fields white tassels unfold. The corn comes up; it comes up green; here upon our fields green leaves blow in the breeze. Blue evening falls, blue evening falls; near by, in every direction, it sets the corn tassels trembling. The wind smooths well the ground. Yonder the wind runs upon our fields. The corn leaves tremble. On Tecolote fields the corn is growing green. I came there, saw the tassels waving in the breeze, and I whistled softly for joy. Blowing in the wind, singing, am I crazy corn? Blowing in the wind, singing, am I laughing corn? The night moves, singing. Not sleepy, I. A stick I cut to represent the corn. Where I find the yellow bees there will be much corn."[5]

The "crazy corn" and the "laughing corn" were ears that had colored kernels. Precisely how the singers interacted with the corn and the powers responsible for its growth is not clear, but it seems likely that the singing was more than a magical rite. Most likely it expressed the petition and hope of the people for a good harvest. Many native peoples have not only talked to animals and plants but have also sung to them. Generally singing is considered more powerful than ordinary speech, no doubt because it more fully engages the personality. In native rituals singing often takes on the repetitive, mesmerizing patterns of chanting, helping the spirit move free of the body so that it can "travel" to visionary locales. It is nearly automatic to join the singing to dancing and drumming, the better to impress the message into every fiber and nerve. Singing to their corn, the Papago might often have traveled out to commune with its spirit, which we might speculate was the general spirit of fecundity, the generally mysterious ability of nature to produce food, specified to the particular case of corn. The singing would have been esthetic, religious, and magical (an effort to shape mysterious powers to human volition) all in one. It would have gladdened the people's hearts, not only because music generally is soothing, but also because it carried the hopes and fears pent up in their breasts.

For the Navaho, the beauty of the earth was the linchpin of any sane person's worldview. The following chant expresses the ideal relationship people would establish with the earth:

"The Earth is looking at me; she is looking up at me. I am looking down on her. I am happy. She is looking at me. I am happy. I am looking at her. The Sun is looking at me; he is looking down on me. I am looking up at him. I am happy. He is looking at me. I am happy. I am looking at him. The Black Sky is looking at me; he is looking down on me. I am looking up at him. I am happy. He is looking at me. I am happy. I am looking at him. The Moon is looking at me; he is looking down on me. I am looking up at him. I am happy. He is looking at me. I am happy. I am looking at him. The North is looking at me; he is looking across at me. I am looking across at him. I am happy. He is looking at me. I am happy. I am looking at him."[6]

The repetition of the song makes the theme of mutual openness or perspicuity between human beings and the elements of the earth cause for great human happiness. To be perceived by the earth, the sun, the sky, the dark sky, the moon, and the north is to be kept in being, probably even to be cherished, by the awesome, admirable forces regulating the Navaho world. The singer is happy to live in mutual regard with such forces. The implication might be that those with disturbed consciences would not be so happy to be completely open to the sky and the earth, the sun and the moon. In terms of Navaho ideals, however, knowing these powers, and being known by them, is the quintessence of the good spiritual life. It is the contemplation and communion that make the people flourish.

Moreover, the accent of this contemplation and communion is more than economic or practical. It is what the earth and the sky are, more than what they give, that holds center stage. Certainly the Navaho need the food that the earth gives, the light, warmth, and rain of the sky, but even more they need to know that these powers are observing them, interested in their situations, engaged with them in a common enterprise.

Why should conviction about such a common enterprise make the Navaho happy? Here we enter the inner precincts of all human prayer, biblical and eastern as well as Native American. Saint Augustine said that our hearts are restless until they rest in God. Other saints, from other traditions, have said much the same: the most basic human vocation is to commune with ultimate reality, divinity, the love that moves the stars. One can achieve all sorts of worldly success, miss such communion, and so feel hollow and perhaps be a sad failure. One can possess few worldly goods and honors, yet occasionally feel the ineffable touch of divinity, and find existence surpassingly good. No healthy people despises the goods of creation, least of all a people that lives in intimate contact with nature. But neither does any healthy people make the goods of creation or human provenance the measure of the human heart or vocation. Not only does our reach exceed our grasp, but our hearts are restless for what eye has not seen and ear does not hear, what it has not entered the human mind to conceive. The good things God has stored up for those who love God are intimated in the moments of ecstasy, when the beauty of the world becomes a blessing upon one's own soul. They are also intimated in the moments of endurance, when despite great pain and darkness one seems carried by a puff of grace and is enabled to let go, to trust that somehow, some day, all will be well. These are the crucial and paradigmatic moments of human existence, when one is attuned to the invitation of divinity to commune with it. Native Americans such as the Navaho were finely attuned to that invitation, so much of their prayer rang with a primordial happiness.

RITUALS

The ritualistic life of most Native American tribes has been rich with songs, chants, dances, and costumes. Many of the tribes have used masks to liberate the participants and ease the entry of spirits into their midst. For example, what scholars call the "false face" masks of the Seneca stand out as especially impressive. The Seneca sponsor a men's society who wear such masks when performing at ceremonies for New Year's day and the green corn. The intent of the men's performances is to ward off the effects of witches and disease. In the background of this usage is the Seneca mythology of the creation of the world. The agents of creation were twins, one of whom produced the good forces while the other produced the evil forces. When seeking a blessing on such a crucial time as New Year's day or the arrival of the green corn, and also when engaged in healing ceremonies, the Seneca would don the masks to handle the legacy of the Bad Twin, the forces of evil.

The Seneca masks are carved from the trunk of a basswood tree and painted black and red. Usually they have large eyes, the metal pupils of which have been exaggerated. The nose and mouth typically are large to the point of being grotesque. Huge teeth, a pendulous tongue, and long hanks of hair complete the typical mask.

If we delve into the Seneca mentality expressed in the masks, we find that

". . . these masks are carved by a member of the Society of Faces and modeled upon a dream revelation. In a man's dream, the appearance of the face of his guardian spirit is revealed, and he carves the mask to make manifest that spirit. The faces when carved are considered to be alive and are treated accordingly by their custodians. When not in use, they are hung facing the wall or wrapped and carefully placed in a box or drawer. Periodically they are fed by smearing on their lips a thick gruel of parched cornmeal and maple sugar. They are also occasionally wiped with sunflower-seed oil 'to keep their skin soft.' Old masks shine from many applications of oil. Each mask is named and has a personality of its own. They are talked to, sung to, and addressed as 'grandfather.' The 'faces' are considered highly potent, for they manifest the powers of the Bad Twin who, when overcome by the Good Twin at the close of creation, was destined to aid in keeping the health and well-being of human beings.

"In this example, we see that the face is not a mask at all, in the sense of being a covering or a disguise. Nor is it false in any sense. The faces are the living manifestation of a type of spiritual being revealed through dreams made manifest in the form of living wooden faces. The wearing of the face is not to cover or disguise the wearer; it is to present and animate the real presence of the spirit."[7]

Although the face is worn to present the real presence of the spirit of a power of the Bad Twin, in fact it does disguise the identity of the wearer and so facilitate a twofold liberation. The wearer is liberated psychologically, being freed to identify with the spirit represented and so to extend his experience of how such a spirit may operate in the world. The wearer is also liberated socially, in that those observing the ceremony tend to react to him in his persona of spirit rather than his everyday persona. The two liberations feed one another, so that the ceremony becomes a privileged experiential zone, a patch of space and time where the rules of ordinary life may be suspended.

In most significant religious rituals, such a suspension of workaday reality is important. The Jewish ritual for Passover tries to take those involved back to the moment of the Exodus. Such an imaginative journey or recall amounts to what liturgical scholars call an *anamnesis*: a profound remembrance of the paradigmatic roots of one's faith and peoplehood. Similar dynamics are at work in the Christian eucharist, where, contrary to the evidence of the senses, one believes that bread and wine represent the body and blood of Christ. The more a given people lives in the mythopoeic world facilitated by nonliteracy, the more such remembrances and reenactments tend to be absorbing. It is easier for oral peoples to travel out of themselves, because they have fewer intermediaries between their consciousnesses and the hypothetical worlds that stories, symbols, sights, sounds, dances, drummings, and the like can summon up. A consciousness formed by texts and literate traditions tends to control the flights of the imagination and feelings, tethering both faculties to what is rational, customary, prudent. The Native American world generally was more expansive, willing to entertain more possibilities, when it came to estimating how the truly significant world of the spiritual forces responsible for life and death, good fortune and ill fortune, functioned.

We should also note what one might call the exorcizing function of the Seneca faces. Inasmuch as they represented forces associated with the Bad Twin and bearing on illness, coopting them into rituals designed to ward off evil influences probably was a stroke of psychological genius. Using the sort of negation of a negative that psychoanalytic thinkers treasure, the face-wearers were assuring the onlookers that all ultimately was well, because the most fearsome forces had been brought into the battle on their side. In effect, they were making present the actors of their worst nightmares, or at least of their most challenging mythology, and assuring the onlookers that these had come under ritualistic control. By confronting their bogies, the face-wearers and onlookers alike could cut them down to size.

Speaking about his own Hopi religious ceremonies, which feature the use of kachina masks and costumes, Emory Sekaquaptewa has indicated the important role the kachinas play in a child's passage to adulthood, and also how the kachinas mediate the typical Hopi's lifelong effort to penetrate ever more deeply into the spiritual world that is the tribe's most abiding interest. The key moment in the child's maturation comes when he or she is allowed to don a kachina mask and participate in tribal ceremonies, for at that moment the child has to make the transition from believing in the kachinas literally to living with them as human impersonations of spiritual forces.

As Sekaquaptewa himself puts it,

"Since the kachina has been so prominent in the child's life, most of the child's fantasies have involved the kachina. Before his initiation most of his fantasies have consisted in emulating the kachina. Children go around the corner of the house; they enact their feelings about the kachina, they dance and sing like the kachina. At this early age they begin to feel the sense of projection into spiritual reality. When the child is initiated and becomes eligible to participate as a kachina, it is not difficult to fantasize now as a participant in the real kachina ceremony, and that is the essence of the kachina ceremony. The fantasizing continues, then, in spite of the initiation which seems to have the effect of revealing to the child that this is just a plaything, now that we are grown up and we don't believe. The idea of make-believe continues with the Hopi man and woman as they mature, and as far as I am concerned it must continue throughout life. For the kachina ceremonies require that a person project oneself into the spirit world, into the world of fantasy, or the world of make-believe. Unless one can do this, spiritual experience cannot be achieved.

"I am certain that the use of the mask in the kachina ceremony has more than just an esthetic purpose. I feel that what happens to a man when he is a performer is that if he understands the essence of the kachina, when he dons the mask he loses his identity and actually becomes what he is representing . . . the essence of the kachina ceremony for me as a participant has to do with the ability to project oneself into the make-believe world, the world of ideas and images which sustain that particular representation."[8]

Not all Native American rituals have involved masks or impersonating spiritual forces, but the majority have, because the majority of Native American rituals have amounted to excursions into the spiritual world. To heal a sick person, consecrate a newly born child, send a dead person to the next life, petition rain, or give thanks for a successful hunt or harvest, one has to break out of the merely human realm, the Native American equivalent of the secular, and either travel to the realm of the spirits responsible for human fate or import such spirits into the human realm. Usually, both traveling and importing took place. The person dancing in the garb of a kachina was exiting ordinary reality and entering the world of greater spiritual possibilities that the kachinas inhabited. At the same time, the physical presence of the kachinas in human beings' midst made clear their contact with, perhaps even their stake in, human affairs. The genius of the typical oral culture, Native American, African, European, or Asian, has been to engage the entire personality— body, spirit, and social malleability—in the exchanges with the spiritual world that the typical tribe considered the basic coin of meaning. To gain sense and significance—to take hold of birth and death, disease and health, good fortune and bad fortune— traditional peoples have had to enact the dramas such factors implied. Instinctively, they have felt that the really real, the sacred, both transcends ordinary human existence and intersects with it. Their rituals have been the major way they have expressed such a feeling, and inasmuch as their rituals drew their best artistic skills, most traditional peoples have loved their key ceremonies as the most beautiful and meaningful moments in their calendar year or life-cycle.

CHRISTIAN REFLECTIONS

As is true of the other religious traditions we have treated, Native American traditions have been immensely more complex than we have been able to indicate. No doubt because he sensed that his treatment of the religion of the American Indians was bound to founder on the shoals of such complexity, the esteemed historian of religions Ake Hultkrantz went out of his way at the beginning of his major work to acknowledge the dangers of suggesting a simple unity in Native American religious traditions:

"It is only from a superficial perspective that the American Indian religions constitute a unity. They do not evince specific traits that set them apart from the tribal religions of the Old World, unless that strength of mind should be mentioned which has been expressed in severe asceticism and individualism. Furthermore, Indian religions form such a changing mosaic that it is difficult to discern a common background. We must never forget that America is a spacious double continent and that it once housed hundreds of languages and thousands of ethnic groups whose religious peculiarities varied as much as European religions before the introduction of Christianity. It is easy to illustrate this by adducing some examples from North America: the simple hunting religion of the Naskapi Indians of Labrador contrasts sharply with the intricate horticultural religion of the Pueblo Indians of New Mexico and Arizona, and the simple structure of the Californian Indian religions bears little resemblance to the religion of sacred kingship represented by the Natchez on the lower Mississippi. Even among tribal religions of the same type the nature of conceptions and rites has varied. The more our research is concerned with taking stock of tribal Indian religions the richer and more complicated becomes our picture of their total outcome."[9]

The relevance of this confession for our study of prayer is direct, because prayer always presupposes and expresses a comprehensive cultural setting. So the prayers of the Navaho could vary significantly from the prayers of the Papago, because the Navaho and Papago cultures differed significantly. The same would hold for any comparison of the prayers or rituals or myths of the Lakota and the Navaho or the Lakota and the Papago. This said, however, it still seems legitimate to ask what a summary, generalizing statement about Native American prayer would present as the characteristic essence, all the while realizing that any such statement probably would require great qualifications for some tribes and might often obscure the actual reality of prayer.

In such a summary statement, the place of the physical world certainly would loom large, and probably one would want to stress the impact that natural beauty regularly has made on the Native American psyche. Many tribes could muster distinctions between the physical world and the spiritual powers responsible for its rise and structure, but few tribes developed such distinctions into a metaphysics that stressed divinity's transcendence of the world. Rather, Native American divinity has tended to be coextensive with the forces manifested in the physical world, as well as in the psychic world peculiar to human beings, and present through them. One might generalize about such forces and collect them in a concept such as *Wakan-Tanka,* the holy ultimate, but more often Native Americans would pray to or with specific localizations of such holiness. As we have noted, regularly Native American prayer has utilized the four directions of the compass. Equally, it has drawn on the benevolent power manifested in grass, wood, smoke, steam, light, and warmth. The animals with which a given tribe regularly interacted furnished it many motifs for prayer, as did the mountains, desert, or waters peculiar to the tribe's geographical region. And although evil certainly intruded into Native American prayer sufficiently to make witchcraft, disease, and death important topics, the more profound instinct of the prayers that make their way into anthologies is to bless the divinities for the goodness of the world. It is the world, the natural expanse of sky and earth, mountain and stream, that is ordered and human beings that require ordering. The world is the constant, the reliable factor, while hu-

good quote

man beings are the variable, twisted factor that prayer must make constant and straight.

Thus, much Native American prayer has been like some Japanese prayer in assuming that nature is closer to divinity (buddhanature) than human beings. What nature achieves spontaneously — being its complete, whole, perfect self — human beings must struggle to achieve. By contemplating nature, and recognizing the gifts of divinity to it, human beings may be humbled, softened, and instructed in ways that ease their growth to whatever maturation they may finally achieve.

The point for Christians wanting to broaden their conception of prayer might be the "ecological" overtones. Frequently discussions of the roots of the ecological crisis (the pollution of nature) conclude that what is at issue is spirituality: how people orient themselves in the world and think about creation. Sometimes theologians have recognized that Christianity contributed to the conflict between modern technology and nature. In doing this, not only did Christian faith risk nurturing an anthropocentrism out of line with the facts about human beings' place in the universe, but it also risked forgetting the divine presence in all of creation. As a consequence, few Christians got the full encouragement to incorporate nature into their prayer that they might have gotten, had the beauty and vastness of the physical world been promoted as holy presences of God. At the least, then, people who admire Native American prayers that treat nature with much fellow-feeling may go and do likewise with their Christian traditions. They need only take a fresh look at the Psalms, for example, to find biblical warrants for sending toward God in prayer the awe, admiration, wonder, and other emotions that the contemplation of the natural world tends to stimulate.[10]

We should also note that many Native American tribes have incorporated Christian religious notions and so now possess hybrid religious cultures. Some scholars tend to shy away from this fact, preferring to deal with Native American traditions as though they were pristine, unmarked by nearly five hundred years of contact with whites, but the price of such an option can be disregarding the actual religious reality that many Native Americans now experience.

Carl Starkloff, a Christian missionary whose admiration of Native American traditions is beyond doubt, has put the matter in these terms:

"Among the Pueblo there exist, side by side, the various native cults and a fully traditional Catholicism, with certain syncretic practices tolerated or even encouraged by the church authorities. What subtle influences one tradition may have had on another can be judged only by those with firsthand acquaintance. The peyote religion, as is well known, is one of the most enthusiastic of Jesus cults. His name figures in their prayers and He is symbolized by the plant itself, being made present by its 'power.'

"The Sun Dances of the Arapaho and the Shoshone are now filled with Christian traits. It is believed by some ethnologists that the influence of the Episcopal bishop John Roberts can be seen in the works of charity and gifting that occurs in the Shoshone celebrations (although this could also be related to Arapaho custom), as well as the great attention paid to God as personal Creator and Father. Arapaho Offerings Lodge worshipers can be seen to wear scapulars, rosaries, and medals about their necks, and Christian symbols on their beaded aprons. . . . Some purists may pejoratively call all of this syncretism, but to do so would be to deride the testimony of the centuries and the cultures from Syria to Gaul to the New World which have influenced Christian teaching and ritual and intertwined with it to create new indigenous forms of church worship. Rather than mock such 'syncretism,' one might encourage these native additions as genuine worship, while advocating (as do many peyote leaders today) participation in the usual forms of Christian devotion and education."[11]

One might also urge that those wishing to pass judgment on a particular worship service take as their first interest the quality of spirit expressed. By "the quality of spirit" we mean the intention of those worshiping, the degree of their desire to praise the goodness of God and receive from that goodness the healing (faith, hope, love) their honesty moves them to confess they need. To say this is not to minimize the importance and utility of accurate forms for expressing orthodox faith. It is rather to remind ourselves that "orthodoxy" means "right praise" as well as "right opinion." What has been the desire at the foundations of the typical Native American (or, for that matter, the typical Jewish, Muslim, Hindu, or Buddhist) liturgical ceremony? When Native Americans have tried to measure up to the best in their traditions of worship, how have they thought and felt about themselves and the world? If one can find evidence that they have wanted to praise the source of the world as the repository of all their hopes and the likely source of the best in them, one can say that divine grace has surely been manifest. If one can say that divine grace surely has been manifest, one can also say, "Amen."

Chapter 7

AFRICAN RELIGIONS

BACKGROUND

The problem of diversity that bedevils the study of Native American religions returns when it comes to studying the religions of Africa. One recent introduction to African religions puts the matter in this way:

"What is the context for the religious traditions we shall be examining? How can the dark continent become illumined for us? We shall start by learning something about the realities of Africa. Africa is the second largest of the continents on our planet. Its actual population today is estimated to be about four hundred million [the 1989 Yearbook of the Encyclopaedia Britannica estimates 606 million]. The land consists of thick forests, high plateaus covered with tall grasses and acacia trees, and severe deserts. An astonishing variety of human societies occupy its land areas, and a wide range of languages reverberate on its streets and pathways. In the Niger-Congo language family alone there are nine hundred languages, each having numerous dialects; the Bantu languages, each consisting of many forms, are only one subgroup of this vast array of languages in the Niger-Congo family."[1]

Another introductory survey of African religions, while equally impressed by the diversity of African cultures, is more sanguine about an underlying cultural, and so religious, unity:

"Having looked at the diversity of African peoples and their religions, we now come to the other side of the 'many but one' paradox. . . . Because these tribes share the same experience of being small-scale, 'closed' societies with a simple technology, they also share a *common world view* which underlies their religious practices and beliefs. This common world view is implicit, not explicit. That is, African peoples do not write discourses on the nature of humanity or the problem of the knowledge of God as modern theologians do. They do not consciously systematize their beliefs. Instead, they experience religious ritual, they transmit myths which explain the nature of things through stories about gods, they use proverbs which contain folk wisdom, and they consult diviners who apply the beliefs of the tribal religion to the practical dilemmas of sickness and suffering. Underlying all these teachings and experiences is an implicit philosophy. Some scholars who have studied African religions for the past decades have found that behind the various rituals, gods, practitioners, and spirits in all of these local religions lies a remarkable uniformity in the various peoples' understanding of the nature of the world, the nature of human beings and their place in the world, and the nature of evil. It is these understandings which comprise what might be called the primal world view."[2]

The move from diversity of languages, cultural systems, and rituals to some likeness or unity in basic worldview seems correct. Part of such unity no doubt comes from the cultural interactions of many tribes. Another part comes from likeness in natural habitat. But the major source of unity in African religions, as in the world religions generally, is the constancy of human nature or the human predicament. Despite great linguistic and cultural diversity, all human beings die, experience ignorance, and have to grope for the meaning of their lives. No ritualistic or doctrinal system, no matter how elaborate or effective, can block out the mysteriousness of the physical world, the human heart, or the fate that awaits human beings after death. Religion grows from such roots, so religion always is implicated at the depths of the human condition. What similarities across the continent mark African religions as a distinctive family derive from the emphases characteristic of African responses to death, ignorance, and mystery. We may initially experience such common African customs as animal sacrifice or divination as foreign to our modern Western experience, but when we penetrate the intention of such customs they quickly seem familiar. Sacrifice usually is an effort to honor the powers thought responsible for human fate and right some imbalance or disharmony that human behavior has introduced into people's relations with such powers. Divination is usually a search for either the cause of a present misfortune or the pattern in which future events are likely to unfold. Neither practice is limited to African religions, and both assume the reality of a world of spiritual forces usually not perceptible to the human senses—an assumption we have found many other religious traditions to make. So even though the particulars of African mythology, ritual, or prayer may strike us as distinctive and irreducible, the reasons why Africans have generated their stories, ceremonies, and prayers are common enough to make such religious practices familiar, even attractive.

The history of the African peoples of course is as complicated as the temporal map showing how the so many different tribes arose and developed their present cultures. Paleontologists now generally agree that Africa is the most likely site for the rise of our human species, and while estimates of the date at which true *homo sapiens* arose vary considerably, all authorities agree that that date lies millions of years before Christ. The custom nowadays is to divide Africa into two main regions, the sub-Sahara and the region above (north of) the Sahara. To the north, Islam has made a great impact. On the rest of the continent, Christianity has become a major factor. But throughout Africa native, pre-Muslim and pre-Christian, traditions have remained influential, even when a given tribe or ethnic family has become Muslim or Christian. With Islam and Christianity have come many features of originally Arab or European cultures, but the majority of the African population continues to resist complete Westernization, preferring to incorporate Western or Muslim features into its older African substance.

In terms of the natural economies that have shaped traditional African religions, commentators sometimes divide the continent into three zones. To the north both hunting and pastoral life (grazing animals) have been traditional. In the central third, farming tropical crops (tubers) has long been important. In the southern third, hunting and gathering was the rule until perhaps 2000 years ago. Areas north of the equator probably passed from hunting and gathering to the controlled production of food about 6000 years ago. Areas south of the equator, which tended to be cut off from technological developments in the north by the marshes of the Nile and the great rain forests, only acquired the technology associated with the Iron Age about 2000 years ago.

"From the sixth and fifth millennia B.C.E. domestic cattle and cereals came into northern Africa from western Asia. In the third millennium B.C.E. the Sahara area shifted from its previous wet phase and dessicated, pressuring pastoralists to penetrate the jungles of the Nile valley. Perhaps 3500 years ago people were growing such tropical grains as millet and sorghum in central Africa, and there may have been marginal cultivation of fruits and vegetables in the forest zones. Stone Age farmers appear to have penetrated the forests of eastern Africa and spread from Ethiopia into central Kenya and northern Tanganyika about 2500 years ago. At about the time when iron started to transform the African economy, 2000 years ago, fishing was probably a major occupation, with some horticulture on the margins, for people could fish in the forests using the waterways of the Congo system.

"In ancient Egypt, however, bronze was used from the late fourth millennium B.C.E., and after the Assyrians used iron weapons in their invasion of Egypt in 663 B.C.E. the use of iron spread rapidly. Thus, from the sixth century B.C.E., more than 2500 years ago, the capital city of the Kingdom of Kush, Meroe, was a center of ironworking. Carthaginians in northern Africa were also working iron in the seventh and sixth centuries B.C.E. After the introduction of the camel from Asia around 100 B.C.E., many inventions, such as ironworking and its products, traveled the Sahara desert more easily."[3]

In modern times the European nations divided up the African continent and increasingly predominated, to the extent that prior to World War II most of Africa was part of European colonial empires. The British and French had the greatest holdings, but Belgium, Italy, and Germany were also significant powers. After World War II revolutionary movements spread across the continent, creating a pattern of European withdrawal. Intertribal strife, along with massive problems of adapting economically and politically to the late twentieth-century world, has marked many African countries, contributing to widespread poverty and suffering. Numerous new African religions have arisen, partly in response to European cultural influences and partly in response to the challenges of the new times. The droughts afflicting east Africa have produced considerable starvation and malnutrition, while the ideological issues surrounding the apartheid of South Africa have made racism a prominent consideration.

Through all such change, however, Africans have continued to pray, whether in traditional tribal formulas and settings or in new Muslim, Christian, or syncretistic usages. And despite the cultural upheaval that many Africans have suffered, especially African intellectuals, the majority of the people living outside the cities have continued to venerate their ancestors, consider dreams sources of revelation, pursue rites of psychosomatic healing, fear the possibility of witchcraft, think of good health and vitality as primary signs of divine blessing, venerate the beauty of their familiar mountains, forests, and rivers, and consider the life-cycle best guided by traditional rites of passage.

STORIES

Stories have proliferated throughout African cultures as the primary way people have interpreted the world and amused themselves. Many of the stories bear directly on matters of religious consequence, such as the origin of the present shape of the world. One of the problematic aspects of the present shape of the world frequently has been why God and the heavens are so far away. Originally, many tribes have suspected, there was no great separation and communication with God was easy. The Margi of Nigeria say that once upon a time human beings could reach up and touch the sky. That was a blessed time, when life was easy and there was no need to work. God would fill the calabashes (gourds) of human beings with all the food they needed. One day, however, a woman put out a dirty calabash that infected the finger of one of the sky children. That angered God, causing him to withdraw. Another version of the story is that a woman hit the sky with her pole while pounding grain, while a third version says that some women took pieces of the sky and broke them into the soup they were making.

In each case, a kind of "original sin" caused God to withdraw in anger or hurt. The implication is that human beings somehow have deserved the separation from heaven they now suffer. The fact that these stories make women the agents of the primordial rupture probably is significant. Just as the patriarchal Israelites developed a tradition in which Eve, the first woman, was the initiator of the fall, so many patriarchal African tribes have blamed the distance of heaven on women. Geoffrey Parrinder, whose sketch of African myths of origin we have been following, is explicit in linking many African intuitions to the biblical intuitions expressed in the Genesis story of the garden of Eden:

"Rather like the Garden of Eden story is that of the Mende, who say that God once lived in a cave and invited the animals to come in pairs but forbade them to touch his food. One day the cow smelt the sweet-smelling food and ate some, and at once God seized the animal and threw it out of the cave. The monkey and all the animals eventually sinned and suffered the same fate, including man. Now all the animals wander about looking for that delicious food, and God watches them from above. Men did not pray at first, until God gave them a mountain whose voice they could hear. The Dogon of South Mali also say that God originally had no altars, but he came in the guise of a beggar asking for drink, and the good man who received him was shown how to make an altar."[4]

Common to these stories is the instinct that something is wrong with an order in which creatures have to search out their food, worry about the morrow, and feel alienated from God. The voice of the mountain that helped people pray could have been volcanic, or simply the thunder that is so impressive in mountain storms. Mountains regularly function in traditional religions as places God is likely to inhabit, because of their apparent closeness to heaven. In some accounts of human origins the original condition was one of such closeness between Creator and creatures that prayer (by which tribal peoples often mean petition) was not necessary. The necessity of prayer that human beings experience nowadays therefore is another sign of their fallen condition. On the other hand, the Dogon apparently link religion (the altar) with human goodness, suggesting that prayer is a good thing. As well, they apparently link religion and human goodness with treating beggars as though they might be heavenly visitors.

The point to studying African mythology of course is that the stories in people's heads condition how they think about their prayers. Just as Western rituals situate liturgical prayer in the context of the biblical narratives that Westerners use as their paradigmatic religious stories, so Africans and other traditional peoples have prayed in terms of how they thought the world was made, what they believed about the history of the relations between themselves and the god they were addressing, how they understood sickness to have arisen and the gods to have prescribed curing it, and so forth.

Concerning death, for example, a wealth of African myths has shaped African funerary rites. For instance, one popular account of the origin of death says that God wanted to tell human beings that they would not die, so he sent a message with a dog. The dog tarried along the way, however, so another animal came first with the message that human beings *would* die. Believing this, human beings buried their corpses, making it impossible to raise the dead back to life. This common story admits of many variations, in some of which the lazy animal messenger is punished. In a version that has the hare as the messenger, for instance, the hare is punished by having its lip split. In another version, the chameleon is punished by having human beings constantly try to chase it away, which necessitates its having to change its color to escape detection. The interesting point to this complex of stories about the origin of death is the accidental, casual character of the misfortune. What sort of a world is it if a simple mistake can lead to such a momentous result? One answer to this question has been that it is the sort of world in which one should be very cautious not to make mistakes. When such a caution is combined with elaborate ritual, the result can be religious ceremonies heightened by a sense that great stakes are at issue and considerable fear is warranted.

The BaMbuti of the Congo have many stories related to the forest in which they live. Some of these stories explain why on many nights they sing to the forest, using long tubes to make their songs hauntingly resonant. The ceremonial singing, which, like the tubes themselves, is called the molimo, expresses the people's love of the forest and gratitude to it for all the good things of BaMbuti life. Thus Moke, an elder of the tribe, explained to the anthropologist Colin Turnbull the blank check the BaMbuti gave to the forest:

"Normally everything goes well in our world. But at night, when we are sleeping, sometimes things go wrong, because we are not awake to stop them from going wrong. Army ants invade the camp; leopards may come in and steal a hunting dog or even a child. If we were awake these things would not happen. So when something big goes wrong, like illness or bad hunting or death, it must be because the forest is sleeping and not looking after its children. So what do we do? We wake it up. We wake it up by singing to it, and we do this because we want it to awaken happy. Then everything will be well and good again. So when our world is going well then also we sing to the forest because we want it to share our happiness."[5]

This story illustrates the faith of an elderly man, who has seen all the permutations of BaMbuti life, but who believes that at all times the forest is good. If bad things happen, that is accidental—due to some unusual gap in the providential care the forest usually furnishes. The greatest joy in BaMbuti life is to commune with the forest. The nightly choruses of the molimo are like a lover's concert: music sent forth tenderly. Certainly the BaMbuti use the molimo to move themselves closer to the roots of their selfhood, which sink deeply into the Congo forest. But they also think of the forest as the best representative of the divinity they know no one can picture or explain. Singing to the forest therefore gives them an ikonic, sacramental way of focusing their minds and hearts on the ultimate mystery they sense must be holding them in being.

Turnbull loved the BaMbuti, whose life in the forest was relatively comfortable. He did not like the Ik, another tribe he studied, because their traditional way of life in the mountains along the border of Uganda and Kenya had been disrupted by international politics, bringing them close to starvation and cultural collapse. In their collapsed state, they seemed nasty to one another, doubly nasty to outsiders, and thoroughly cynical. Nonetheless, some vestiges of their original mythology remained— enough to suggest happier times, when relations with the ancestor beings had been easier. From some old ritual priests, Turnbull learned that the sky god Didigwari created the world but then retreated from it to the recesses of heaven. That meant shifting focus to the ancestors likened to the many stars in the night sky:

"The *abang*, or ancestors, are often likened to the stars; they are as numerous and as widely scattered, as ever changing and as quietly watchful. Every now and then one descends to earth again for some unknown purpose, but mostly, like Didigwari, they are remote and can be approached only by the great ritual priests. ... Didigwari never came down to earth, but the abang have all known life on earth, so it is only against them that one can sin, and only to them that one can turn for help, through the ritual priest. If the abang are angered they will punish: they can send hunger, they can kill."[6]

Along with their diminished cultural condition, the Ik had suffered a parallel diminishment in the memory and efficacy of their traditional mythology and ritual life. The three components of culture—economics, mythology, and ritual—had been so interrelated that when the Ik were forbidden the right to follow their cattle across new national boundaries they became spiritually impoverished. Something cynical arose from the fissure in their traditional culture, and this caused them to doubt the significance of the old stories and rites. The absence of the high creator god—a regular theme in African mythology—lost the positive connotations of "mystery," becoming entirely privative: God was of little if any account. This reminds us how pragmatic many tribal religions have been: if a mytho-ritualistic complex was not working, the gods it celebrated and the priests it employed quickly came under scrutiny, even attack. African prayer, as much other "primitive" (aboriginal, vigorous) spirituality, has been as concrete and practical as getting one's next meal and enjoying a healthy, fertile body.

PRAYERS

The majority of African prayers have been petitions for blessing and fertility, although sometimes Africans have been carried away in pure praise of the source of the beauty and fecundity of their lands. A prayer to Imana, the creator venerated by the Ruanda-Urundi, illustrates the heartfelt petition of a person in sore distress: "Give me offspring, give me as you give to others! Imana, what shall I do, where shall I go? I am in distress, where is there room for me? O Merciful, O Imana of mercy, help this once."[7]

The prayer for offspring, probably uttered by a woman but perhaps by a man, is reminiscent of the prayer of the biblical Hannah (I Sam. 1:11), who was heartsick because barren. Fertility often figures in African rituals as a mark of divine blessing, so being without children could seem a mark of divine disfavor. Indeed, in most tribal cultures children represent security, as well as foci of love. Not to be blessed with numerous healthy children is to worry about one's old age, as well as the continuance of one's line.

The person making this prayer implies a comparative basis for complaint: Imana has been treating other people quite well; why should she or he not receive equal prosperity? The final verses of the prayer illustrate a regular feature of all peoples' prayer: God is the final recourse, in two senses. First, people may only petition a god when they have exhausted their own ingenuity and other sources of help. Second, and more significantly, "God" functions as the one to whom nothing is impossible, the one who can overturn the misfortunes allowed by all lesser forces. Few functions or implications of prayer have been more important than this one of providing ultimate recourse. By giving people access to the mysterious depths of creation, prayer has regularly kept hope alive. As long as hope is alive, people will keep struggling, and as long as people keep struggling their fortunes may change, opening the possibility that at the end of their lives they may be able to bless what has happened to them as necessary and in the final analysis good.

"A hymn to Mwari, God of the Mashona of southern Zimbabwe, recites his attributes and accomplishments (he piled the rocks into mountains and sewed the heavens like cloth), then asks a hearing and mercy. A South African bushman asks his God Gauwa for help in hunting, complains that Gauwa is cheating him, but concludes on a note of hope: 'Gauwa will bring something for us to kill next day, after he himself hunts and has eaten meat, when he is full and feeling well.' "[8]

The tendency to preface one's petitions with recitations of God's attributes, perhaps especially those that suggest God will grant the person praying a favorable hearing, runs throughout African as well as biblical prayer. The huntsman who complains that Gauwa is cheating inserts a bold note, perhaps indicative of a special familiarity between his people and their god. One of the regular problems that African prayers encounter is the do-nothing character that God can exhibit. Scholars sometimes have spoken of such a God as "otiose," noting that, because of the distance and lack of response the creator frequently exhibits, many African tribes pay more attention to lesser but closer deities. The ancestor stars figuring in the prayers of the Ik are one example, but other tribes have a richer theology, populating human affairs with gods directing the forces of health and prosperity.

Tribes seem to vary considerably in the frequency with which

they pray. Some groups think of prayer as most fitting in times
of crisis, while others pray every day:

> "It is reported that the Galla make frequent prayers and
> invocations to God. They pray in the morning and evening
> every day, asking Him to protect them, their cattle, their
> crops and their families. One such prayer says: 'O God,
> Thou has given me a good day, give me a good night; Thou
> hast given me a good night, give me a good day!'
>
> "It is also customary among the Barotse to pray every
> day, which old men do, rising up early in the morning and
> making an offering of water to God. They address God as
> the great King to Whom no man can be compared, and
> who shows compassion and innumerable favours to His
> servants. The Illa are said to pray in special need, soliciting
> God's help. When there is a drought, they come together
> and join in singing and invoking God saying, 'Come to us
> with a continued rain, O God, fall!' If men are on a hunting
> expedition and do not kill anything, they sit down round
> the oldest man in the group who leads them in this prayer:
> 'O Mutalabala, Eternal One ... We pray Thee, let us kill
> today before sunset.' The rest, falling to the ground, re-
> spond, 'O Chief, today let us kill!' And when they succeed
> in killing an animal, they cut up the pieces of the meat
> which the oldest man offers to God saying, 'I thank Thee
> for the meat which Thou givest me. Today Thou hast stood
> by me.' "9

Among the Yoruba, and many other tribes, prayers frequently
accompany sacrifices, especially when the prayers are petitions
for help or protection. In one ceremony, focused on the god
Ogun,

> "the festival date is determined through divination in ac-
> cordance with Ogun's wishes. Prior to the event, the Ogun
> priests (Oloode) and the officiating family heads prepare
> themselves morally and physically, so that they may be
> acceptable servants of Ogun. They must abstain from curs-
> ing, fighting, sexual intercourse, and eating certain foods.

The day before the festival begins, the men undertake a hunting expedition in the surrounding bush to gather fresh game. In the evening, an all-night vigil is kept near the compound's Ogun shrine, which consists of a stone column and a tree. Palm fronds decorate the tree on this occasion, for palm wine is Ogun's favorite drink. Throughout the night large quantities of palm wine and beer are consumed by the family members and their guests, and Ogun's special praise chants are sung in honor of the divinity. These songs not only entertain the people, but also attract Ogun's attention and induce him to shower his blessings upon the assembled congregation.

"The sacrifices of the next day begin with an offering of kola nuts brought by each family head on behalf of his wives and children. The kola nuts themselves signify friendship and reconciliation. Presenting them to Ogun at the beginning of the sacrifice establishes an initial bond between the worshipers and the divinity. Setting them before the Ogun stone, each family head, or the Oloode in his stead, asks Ogun for blessings and protection during the year. Since Ogun is the god of iron and steel, he asks especially for Ogun's protection from things made of metal, e.g., from automobiles, bicycles, knives, axes, or guns: 'Ogun, here are Ebun's kola nuts: he rides a bicycle, he cultivates with a machete, he fells trees with the axe. Do not let Ebun meet your anger this year; take care of him. He comes this year, enable him to come next season.' "[10]

No doubt Ogun has prospered as more things made of metal have entered Yoruba culture. The psychomechanics of worshiping a god such as he now involve the advantages of specialization. Inasmuch as a divinity is thought to handle specific functions, people can feel confident that the parts of their lives that fall to that divinity's competence are taken care of. On the other hand, the more complicated people's lives and rosters of divinities, the more complicated their petitionary prayer. If one god takes care of things made of wood and another things made of metal, the need for prayer is doubled.

Nonetheless, many commentators dispute the facile criticisms of "polytheism" that early missionaries and analysts drew from observing Africans praying to diverse deities for diverse needs. Just as Africans and others who have represented divinities with stones or wooden carvings probably have not confused the spiritual divinity with its material symbol, so they have not multiplied deities in such a way as to preclude the possibility of honoring divinity in a comprehensive sense. For many Africans, as for many Native Americans, praying to a particular deity has been a convenient way of localizing and focusing the general relationship between humanity and divinity. The old man Moke, who told Colin Turnbull about the BaMbuti veneration of the forest through the molimo, later made it plain that focusing on the forest was simply a convenient way of dealing with the mysteriousness of God. The BaMbuti did not think that the forest was God pure and simple. But the forest was the best symbol of the comprehensive care and provision they associated with God, so they chose to direct their veneration and love to the forest. In fact no one could know what God was like in himself. God would always remain mysterious. But focusing on the forest (or a localization of God like Ogun) made God imaginable, approachable, in very helpful ways.

Many of these psychomechanics or psychodynamics have exerted great influence in monotheistic religions, despite the claim of such religions to worship a God who is One and completely spiritual. Christians have worshiped an incarnate God, capable of being represented in many different guises, and they have venerated many different saints. Muslims have venerated Muhammad and chanted the many different names of Allah, which have helped to display Allah's omni-relevance. Jews have venerated Torah, the many different lessons of which have applied the divine wisdom to a great diversity of circumstances. As well, both Jews and Muslims have venerated saintly teachers. Certainly, these usages of the monotheistic religions have been only analogous to the usages of peoples whose divinities have not been so clearly One and transcendent of nature, yet they imply that the majority of prayers, in all traditions, have employed images and symbols drawing the deity closer and suggesting the deity's engagement with the problem or desire at hand.

RITUALS

We have seen in the Yoruba ceremony focused on Ogun the fusion of prayer and sacrifice. Many African rituals include the sacrifice (making over to the use of a deity) of something considered valuable, such as kola nuts or an animal. E. E. Evans-Pritchard, writing of Nuer burial practices, notes the inclusion of an animal sacrifice:

"When the burial is completed the master of ceremonies of the dead man's family dips a handful of wild rice in water and asperges the grave-diggers with it. They then go to the nearest stream to wash themselves. They may not drink water before they have been aspersed and have washed lest they die of the consequences. ... A few days later the master of ceremonies sprinkles all the people of the homestead and close kin who live nearby in the same manner and sacrifices an animal to God, an ox if the dead man had a large herd, otherwise one of the flock, in front of the dead man's hut. He also addresses the ghost and tells him that he has been taken away and must turn his face to the ground and not trouble the living: 'Friend, this (beast) is yours (for you). Now turn yourself to the ghosts. Turn yourself away from us. Death was not made by us in old times, it was made by God, friend. Do not trouble your people with bad dreams but regard us favourably. God has not entirely destroyed you, for there are those who come after you; you have children left behind you.' If the family have no animal to sacrifice, the master of ceremonies sacrifices by cutting in two a wild cucumber. 'The half of the living, the half of the children, the right half, remains outside, being placed in the thatch of the hut. The head of the dead man is thrown into the bush.' With it is thrown out of the village the contagion of death. They say of this sacrifice [that] ... 'the dead man is expiated in the earth with a goat,' and that the badness goes into the earth with the blood and the chyme.' "[11]

Rituals such as burial generally serve several different needs. Family members and friends need channels for mourning. The entire tribe has to handle death again. For the Nuer, death is complicated by fears that the ghost of the dead person will be angry and so disturb the living. The sacrifice after burial is a gesture to placate the ghost. The ghost has brought the deceased to a new status, between that of living people and gods. When living people experience dreams of the deceased, they have to take them seriously. In the best of cases, the deceased appear in dreams for benevolent purposes. At any rate, many Africans believe in the efficacy of dreams, the continuing reality of their ancestors, and the value of talking to the deceased. In the latter case, belief often opens the door to therapy and ruminative judgment. Considering a conversation with an ancestor privileged, the living person can derive catharsis and insight from it.

The anthropologist Victor Turner studied intensively the symbols and rituals of the Ndembu of Zambia, finding them rich with overlays of implication. Many of the rituals he studied concerned curing sickness. A person gifted in such curing had high status in Ndembu society:

"Ihembi had been a famous gun-hunter . . . in his youth, and like many such hunters had led a nomadic life which had taken him at various times to the Belgian Congo, to Angola, and to Balovale District in Northern Rhodesia, where he had stayed for many years. He claimed to have practised as a diviner but to have given up this profession after he had been heavily fined by the British Administration, which had made the divining of witches a punishable offense. But Ihembi was everywhere regarded as a great expert in two kinds of curative ritual, and was in constant demand. . . . Both rituals are performed to cure sickness. When either is invoked it is believed that the patient is being afflicted by a mystical agency. *Ihamba* is the name not only of the ritual but also of the afflicting agency, in this case the shade of a dead hunter, which is thought to inhere in one of the two upper front incisors of the dead man. . . . Under the influence of the shade, the tooth is believed to fly about invisibly and to fix itself in the body of a living relative of the hunter. In this way it punishes a person who has failed to pour out a libation of blood or beer to the shade of the deceased, who has 'forgotten the shade in his heart,' or who has offended the shade by quarreling with his kinsfolk. ... The ritual of *Ihamba* ... consists in washing the patient's body with 'medicines' ... pounded leaves, roots, and bark scrapings, giving him medicines to drink, and applying cupping horns ... to his body to 'suck out' ... the hunter's tooth. The tooth, it is believed, tries to avoid capture as long as possible, and travels about beneath the skin of the victim, dodging the cupping horns. Much depends on the moral condition of the patient and of his group in determining whether the hunter's shade will allow the tooth to be removed. The Ihamba ritual is of immense interest to the social anthropologist, since it throws into clear relief many of the current antagonisms in the patient's group. Sometimes, indeed, in the course of an Ihamba ritual, performed for a person occupying a significant position in the social structure of a wider system than the village, the investigator is able to collect material, in the form of prayers, invocations, confessions, comments, and asides, which shows him precisely where the main areas of tension and conflict lie within that system."[12]

Turner's final comments remind us that African rituals regularly serve the function of moderating tensions within groups. One might call them sanctioned ways of ventilating irritations and hatreds. Many African tribes have complicated social organizations, tied to equally complicated concerns for family lineages. These exacerbate the normal tensions of social intercourse, increasing the need for purgative dimensions in religious rituals.

The perhaps bizarre belief in the traveling hunter's tooth is similar to shamanic beliefs in other cultures, where the basic procedure in a healing ritual is to suck from the patient's body a foreign substance believed to cause the distress. Cultures that acknowledge and practice witchcraft frequently associate such a foreign substance with the intent of an enemy to hurt the afflicted person. The belief in such a possibility assures that the removal procedure will be credible, while the impact of such belief can be turned to positive account when the person sees the item supposedly responsible for the illness to have been removed from his or her body. If African curative rituals prove anything, it is the holistic character of native views of health and sickness, and so the immense impact that belief—the psychic side of psychosomatic illness or vitality—can have. Many cases of death from fright—belief in evil forces such as witchcraft— have been documented.

Many of the rituals most prized both by anthropologists and their subjects involve the changes of state associated with progress through the life-cycle. The name that has attached itself to such rituals is "rites of passage." Usually the most dramatic rites are those that occur at adolescence, when people pass from childhood to adulthood. For females, this passage is marked dramatically by the menarche. For males, the passage is more arbitrary. In tribal societies both sexes receive the training deemed necessary for assuming adult responsibilities. Usually this training occurs in seclusion and frequently it includes painful trials. Upon completing such trials, the initiate is presented to the community in his or her new state, again with appropriate ceremonies.

Even when a stage of life does not lend itself to ceremonies, tribal people often are sensitive to the transitions it implies. Thus the BaMbuti have been sensitive to the advent and preoccupations of old age, explaining them through the story of the hunter Nzoki:

> "Nzoki was a hunter, an adult. But he grew tired of hunting and increasingly stayed behind in the forest camp when others went off with nets and bows and arrows and spears. Nzoki would just sit in the camp and whittle away at a piece of wood, making nothing in particular, just whatever happened to the piece of wood as he whittled was fine with him, that was what he wanted. He wanted the wood to be something else.
> "Then he took to wandering off into the forest alone, a sure sign of old age. The villagers would have said he was

a witch. And in the forest you could see him sitting beside a river or a stream, staring at his reflection. And as he stared, he whittled away at a piece of wood and let it be whatever it wanted to be.

"One day, the story goes, he slowly touched his feet to the water, one after the other, and whittling away, he waded out into the river, letting his reflection, his other self, come up through his body and disappear into the world he was leaving behind. He whittled and whittled, and he was still whittling when finally he disappeared beneath the surface, never to be seen again. But if you ever have a piece of wood and want it nicely whittled, just go to that spot, at the edge of the Lelo River, and throw it into the water. Nzoki is there, and he will whittle it for you and give it back to you made into just whatever it wanted to be."[13]

CHRISTIAN REFLECTIONS

Two aspects of the story about Nzoki are paramount. First, it portrays old age as a time for reflection, for discovering who one has become. Second, it so stresses the theme of letting the whittled wood become whatever it wanted to be that this theme becomes a metaphor for life itself. Perhaps the BaMbuti instinct is much like that of St. Paul when he discoursed about the potter and the pot (Rom. 9:21): the sovereign freedom of God (destiny, ultimate reality) to work the potential of any creature into something beautiful. Plato also thought about creaturehood along this line, speaking of the divine puppeteer working the strings that determine human destiny (Laws, I, 644d–645b). If old age tends to be the time when people sit back to contemplate the mysterious patterns in which time and human destiny run, its reflections bear on the whole of life nonetheless. In the figure of letting the wood express whatever it has wanted to be, one finds a delicate appreciation of the call on human beings to attend to the strivings of the materials with which they work. Once again, the ecological message is impressive. If our race is to be a good steward of the earth's resources, we will have to pay better attention to the "desires" of the forests, the streams, and hummingbirds.

The central preoccupation of African prayer with health and fertility is not unique in the span of the world's religious, but it is distinctive. Perhaps this is another expression of a profound instinct that a good God has created the world and is whittling it so as to bring out its most cherished potential. On the whole, African religions have not been ascetic, despite the provision in some ritualistic situations for abstinence and sacrifice. On the whole, sexual pleasure, the pleasure of eating and drinking, of dancing and singing, and of harvesting good crops and raising numerous healthy children has been the preferred place for finding God's blessings. Belief in witchcraft and evil spirits has darkened African prayer, making numerous rituals defensive or curative, yet on the whole there has been more sun than rain. In itself, as well as in its implications for African-American Christianity, African religion mounts a strong challenge to tie divinity to vitality. The God worshiped in the majority of African ceremonies is a giver of health, strength, and joy. When these gifts are lacking or failing, Africans go to their divinities to protest, petition, and beg redress. Death, obviously, is the worst of times, because it calls into question the goodness of human existence. But even at the time of death, African prayer has found such positive features to stress as the continuance of the dead person in his or her progeny.

The history of Christian prayer, mirroring the history of Christian doctrine and spirituality, shows a struggle concerning the proper estimate of the divine goodness. Despite the Pauline assertion (Rom. 5:20) that grace has abounded more than sin, many periods of Christian history stressed the penitential aspects of ritual and prayer, under the impact of a pessimistic view of human nature. The basic message both broadcast and received was that human beings should usually have been lamenting their sins, and the main reason for blessing their God ought to have been for the divine forgiveness of such sins. African prayer suggests a healthy corrective to this potentially dolorous Christian spirituality. If people were to thank God for the light of their eyes and the air they breathed, for the desire in their loins and the light of their minds, they would be less inclined to fall into the preoccupation with self that has mottled too much Christian prayer. To be sure, human beings are sinners, so sin is a proper subject for prayer—morning, noon, and night. Yet straightening the twistedness of human behavior does not exhaust the works of God. The need of the recipient has not been the measure of the donation. The love of God poured forth in our hearts by the Holy Spirit has caused all the lilies of the field and counsels trust, letting go of self-centeredness, and pure praise of the divine Creator, as well as lamentation for sin.

The nervousness with which white, European Christianity has approached African spirituality expresses many unresolved feelings and judgments about this matter of vitality and sinfulness. One can never neglect the matter of institutional power and politics, but the deeper issue in discussions about the Christianization of native African healing rites, the degree of native song and dance appropriate at the Christian liturgy, and the possible harmony of native traditions of polygamy with Christian morality seems to go to root differences between the two cultures. One is relatively comfortable with the body and the world, while the other is not. One spontaneously sings and parties, while the other does not. It would be fine to let the two cultures go their own ways. It would be better to put them into friendly dialogue. At the least, however, African Christians should not have to blunt their profound sense of the goodness and power of God running through creation and the human body in order to be accounted faithful followers of Christ. The further implications for evangelization among African-American Christians are not hard to discern. In the ideal ecumenical situation, the diverse Christian churches would be engaged in an ongoing and completely mutual give and take, offering one another new ideas, new appreciations of the riches of Christ, and helpful cautions or corrections. They would share power and resources equally enough to make all of their exchanges—those that encouraged new ideas and those that supplied chastening—free of concerns about superior or inferior churches, richer or poorer congregations, master or slave psychologies.

Prayer is so primordial a religious act that it is bound to express the degree of freedom or constraint in the soul of the praying individual or congregation. If we go to God with hearts atever its modality, the prayer that has risen from human nitation has had something realistic about it, as though the reator had stamped on its bottom, "Made in common sense." othing is less commonsensical than the pretense of the haughty cularist to self-sufficiency. If one is literate enough to read the bituary column, and is informed enough to hear about the latst victim of cancer, one ought to be wise enough to eschew selfifficiency as a hopeless illusion. As soon as one does eschew elf-sufficiency, one is primed for prayer: for asking of an Other e help one's limitations make plain one needs.

But prayer has been much more than simply petition for the elp that human limitations clarify. It has also been the consumation of the thrust of the mind to know and the heart to love. ne's passionate efforts to understand anything significant bout the human condition—the build of nature, the meaning f death and so of life, the proper finality of the self, the order at would make peace and prosperity—lead the mind to come p against walls of mystery. Take a significant human problem vo or three steps beyond the end of its empirical trail and one as exited into mystery—the darkness at the borders of all human consciousness. There, the proper next step can only be vonder, quiet contemplation, and so prayer. As soon as one has ccepted such mysteriousness, one will hear a call to reverence : and appreciate how it is the primordial datum holding the key o human significance. Such reverence and appreciation are high orms of prayer, for they imply the mind's surrender to the most rofound realism: the mind simply does not know the most basic hings about itself or the person it serves; it simply has to open tself to an illumination gratuitously supplied by an Other if it s to find the fulfillment its constitutive drives postulate and so ot be Jean-Paul Sartre's "useless passion."

The same analysis applies to the dynamics of the human eart; only there the issue is even more crucial. For while the uman being can get by with a mind that never realizes its full alling, when the human heart misses the love that is its destiny he entire human entity atrophies and loses its direction. The larkness one finds at the conclusion of the heart's searches is he same as what one finds at the conclusion of the mind's earches, but the heart has more flexibility, more resources for

and minds full of gratitude as well as need, probably it is because we have been free enough to notice the light of our eyes, the air we breathe, the dozen acts of kindness or fidelity on which our social unit depends to get through any given day. Perhaps the closest, nearest, most intimate gift we have from God is our bodily life—our energy, appetite, love, and desire. How well have most schools of Christian prayer spotlighted this gift and made it a central matter of Christian prayer? How comfortable with their bodies and world have the leading Western spiritualities, Christian, Jewish, or Islamic, made their people feel? If the answer is "not very," or "much less than they might," then the leading Western spiritualities have much to learn from African culture and prayer.

This is not to limit African religious achievements to holism and incarnational appreciation, profound as the implication that these two achievements can carry in the Christian scheme of things is. It is not to overlook the dark sides of native African spirituality and the light that biblical revelation can carry in contrast. African prayer sometimes has descended to the level of economics, as prayer has in other traditions. God could become simply a cornucopia, to be addressed much more when the stream of goods was running out than when everyone was drinking up. Yet, once again, the overall balance seems quite positive. The initiations that have paced many traditional Africans through their life-cycles have been passages into deeper wisdom. The person reflecting on the meaning of the face reflected in the stream has not been tied to goods or social roles. The rhythm of nature and the wonder of fertility have kept the typical religious African close to the mysteriousness of all creativity and destiny. The variations in the provisions of nature, the availability of the game, the coming of rain—all of these reminders of the gratuity of vitality have been occasions to humble the human spirit and face the smallness of the human place in the grand scheme of things.

At the end of his masterful survey of African cultural history and anatomy, Ali A. Mazrui has speculated about the African role in the current family of nations:

"There is a strong possibility that the nuclearisation of Africa is the catalyst that could create consternation among the big powers. The very distrust of Africa and its underdevelopment and instability could begin to induce a true recognition that nuclear weapons have to be denied to all if they are to be denied to anyone. The world cannot be divided for long between nuclear Brahmins and non-nuclear Untouchables, between nuclear haves and non-nuclear have-nots. The egalitarian force in world reform demands equalisation. In order to ensure that no one will have nuclear weapons, it may be necessary for a while to ensure that some more countries have them—especially those least trusted with such a responsibility. The world needs a sense of urgency about nuclear weapons. This sense of urgency has not been created by the super-powers' acquisition of more sophisticated arsenals of destruction. Maybe the sense of urgency will be created by too many small countries acquiring nuclear bombs of their own. A nuclear inoculation is needed to shock the world into nuclear immunisation. Muntu, Man, is facing his most complete crisis. He needs a final scare to convince him that the world is indeed a village; that the human race is indeed a family."[14]

Whether or not one agrees with Mazrui's startling proposal, it seems likely that it stems not simply from the resentment of white condescension that Africans regularly feel but also from long-standing love of village, family, and life. African prayer, so much concerned with the earth and the health of the body, is bound to recoil from the prospect of nuclear devastation, as is any other healthy prayer. But the very embodiment of most African prayer can make the African recoil distinctive and impressively wise. What do we want for our bone marrow, our children, the earth? What ought our prayer to produce as political fruits? Many Africans would agree with Mazrui: a world not threatened by nuclear weapons or power, a world more responsive to the Creator who has given it so much life.

Chapter 8

CONCLUSION

THE WORLDWIDE IMPERATIVE TO

Cursory as our survey of some of the major worl has been, it makes clear the omnipresence of prayer. petition, thanksgiving, adoration, sacrifice, and much filled the minds and hearts of people the world over. this imperative to pray come from, and what does i the current encounters among the world religions?

The imperative to pray has come from human fi need, without doubt, but also from the most positive i of human consciousness. Because human beings ever creatures who are mortal, must suffer, are ignorant, pain, everywhere human beings have reached out to one or Something that might help them: draw them mortality, redeem their suffering, enlighten their igno heal their pain. This outreach is as obvious and de the universal human tendency to ask the fates, the fo guardians of luck and destiny for good hunting, farn birthing, and the like. Because we are not our own i human beings have received in the large print of ou a license to ask Whoever or Whatever made us for h times such a request has carried the implication that could have done a better job, or at least a job whose made more sense to us who suffer from them. At c such a request has been quite crass: the ever-outstret of the beggar, the constant self-promotion of the

coping with this darkness. We can love beyond what we can know, at least beyond what we can know with certitude. We can maneuver in the divine darkness, traveling by the trust, hope, and love (desire, admiration) brimming in our breast. And when our longing is taken up by the divine darkness and our thirst is slaked, we know what we have been made for. Surprised by the joy of the love poured forth in our hearts by the divine Spirit, we can never doubt thereafter that we were sure once that there was great meaning and beauty, that once all manner of thing was well.

One could play variations on both of these themes, human need and human peak times, and so round out a full interpretation of prayer as the most basic of the religious acts. For people alert to the mysteriousness of every thing and moment, prayer can be as natural as breathing. One need only accept, say yes, utter thanks to make each positive bit of experience prayerful. One need only accept, say "Help!," utter a plea, to make each negative bit of experience prayerful. We have been made for God, the Other that the world can never contain, so our hearts are restless until they rest in God — until their prayer has been consummated. That is the story told by the world religions in the so many different accents, myths, rituals, and prostrations of their prayers.

If so, what ought the encounters among the world religions that are occurring with increasing frequency today to make of prayer? At the least, they ought to make prayer a significant item on the agendas they fashion when they propose serious dialogue. With action for social justice, prayer composes a complete profile of an adequate, holistic religious regime. Not to discuss social justice would be to slight the agenda of serious dialogue, but so would not discussing prayer. In our opinion, prayer and social justice are more elementary than religious doctrines, which to date continue to get more attention. We mean no disparagement of religious doctrine. One cannot develop the dialogue about prayer or social justice without moving into the reasons each tradition gives for its stances. But unless those stances have been discussed with some thoroughness, the reasons will be more skeletal than full-bodied. Moreover, there is a tendency in academic versions of interreligious dialogue to expatiate endlessly on reasons, ideas, and theories. Accordingly, both prayer and social action receive short shrift. If prayer deserves anything like the significance our survey in this book has accorded it, such a tendency hopelessly misses the mark.

Does this imply that discussion of prayer is enough to place interreligious dialogue on the right foundations (especially if one also provides for social justice)? Not quite. The fully adequate foundation of interreligious dialogue probably has to be not just discussion of prayer (taken as the most distinctively religious act) but also common practice of prayer. Only when the partners to dialogue experience something of the prayer life of their fellow partners will the dialogue be fully grounded.

If one takes to heart a prayer formula or ritual of another religious tradition, bracketing for the moment the theological objections that might come to mind and trusting simply that because others have found this practice sanctifying it is worth trying, most likely the alien character of the tradition in question will be halved immediately. One may still feel the prostration or chant to be foreign, but the process of trying it on, struggling to make it one's own and expressing one's love or need through it, will greatly domesticate it. Just as those who visit a monastic chapel and spend a peaceful half hour learn something immensely important about monasticism, so those who sit in yoga or sacrifice a kola nut or experience the sweat lodge pass over a border and no longer feel complete outsiders. To be sure, just as a half hour in a monastic chapel only illumines a fraction of the monastic experience, so the other passovers we have imagined are only fractional entries into the traditions they serve. But when one is experientially at zero concerning another tradition, to gain a fraction's worth of experience is to make a quantum leap. So, the first lesson we draw from the worldwide imperative to pray is that those serious about interreligious understanding ought to broaden their experience of this imperative by trying on some of the forms of prayer central in traditions other than their native own.

GRACE ABOUNDING

The second lesson we draw is that God has left all peoples lovely traces of the divine mystery and intent. Any spot of the world can trigger reflection about this mystery, and so trigger prayer, because every consciousness that reflects has been moved by divine grace. Divine grace is the favor God has extended human beings in making the divine substance the gist of human fulfillment. The implication of our restless minds and hearts is that the term they pursue is their fulfillment. This term is nothing less than divinity itself. The revealed religions speak of the divine initiatives that have clarified how God is the gist of human fulfillment. Equally, the revealed religions spotlight the unchartable love that tells human beings they need only stop and abide to know for what they have been made. When God quiets and warms the heart, the human being wants nothing more. For the interval of communion with God, nothing created is disturbing. This is the consummate act of grace: to assure the creature, with an immediacy that dispenses with words, that the center does hold, because the center is divinely good.

As human beings all over the globe struggle to make the world fit to live in, they depend on the hope that such grace can be their foundation. Perhaps the majority of such human beings have no adequate language in which to express such a hope or name the experiences that make it credible. Nonetheless, the Spirit of God can be moving in their depths, with sighs too deep for words, accomplishing the crux of salvation. For what is the crux of salvation but the death of despair and the resurrection of faith that God is alive and benevolent? What is the one thing necessary except the real possibility that time may be taken up into eternity and every tear be wiped from our eyes?

With such a real possibility, we can continue to trudge along, trying to meet fairly and squarely the obligations presented each day. With the images of hope that faith in the passover of human success from death to resurrection provides we can keep the end of the process open and gather ourselves to work another day. No one expects God to take from the human lifetime death and suffering. Shocking as they always remain, death and suffering are so obviously part of the human lifetime that most of wisdom consists of learning to become realistic about them. But everyone hopes, in the dark depths of conscience, that death and suffering will not be the final word. Everyone knows that evil and injustice call the goodness of creation and so of the Creator into deep doubt, so everyone demands, in the still, small voice of bedrock honesty, that evil and injustice not be the ultimate victors. The experience of grace that responds to these common human hopes, awarenesses, and demands is the necessary and sufficient condition for living a human life. Whether or not they recognize it, all people depend on such grace. People who pray explicitly depend on it explicitly. People who do not pray or think they cannot pray tend to hope mutely, at the border of despair. And people who despair, to the point of surrender or suicide, usually have not been able to manage their hopes, either imagining them unrealistically or reposing them in something other than the divine mystery.

The prayer that undergirds traditional cultures the world over is the longing that all the words of devotion, petition, ritual, sacrifice, and the rest try to express. The longing is comprehensive — virtually a definition of what the human being is. The efforts to express it are endless, because partial. Meaningful prayer "says" the 1001 things on the mind and in the heart of the person praying. An analogy to sexual union is quite instructive. The contemplative prayer that binds people to the divine mystery from the center of their being, so that heart speaks to heart, is quite like sexual intercourse. The two beings intertwine, giving and receiving themselves. The human partner's possessions, thoughts, and worries fade away, because what such possessions, thoughts, and worries bear upon is nigh. The presence of God, the love of God poured forth in our hearts, is revelation, salvation, and divinization all in one. The illumination we seek, the healing we beg, and the victory over mortality we seek are all given, because God is communicating divine life.

However little we can understand this experience of grace or communicate it in conceptual categories, we can tell from the glow it leaves that it is the pearl of great price. The more we open ourselves by trying to pray deeply, comprehensively, being to being, the more the experience becomes recognizable as the reason for our spirituality. We have a spark in our clay, a breath in our dust. The love of God tells us why. Anything can trigger our awareness of this love of God. Any lovely or trying moment can hint at our vocation. If a beautiful spring day has quickened our juices, we can take it as a hint of the divine fertility. Then, we can cry out in delight, praise the wisdom of God, and gladly join the stream of all creatures seeking to increase, multiply, and return good interest on the investment God has made in them. If physical or emotional pain has worn us down, we can take it as a hint of our need for repair, recreation, salvation, and so as a reminder of our call to ask our redeemer to live for us, cover over our ugliness and sin, make us acceptable to our God.

The prayers, stories, rituals — indeed the entire histories — of the religious communities around the world come into clearest relief when one considers them to be serving the deepest desires of the human heart. Without disputing their ties to economics, politics, the arts, or the sciences, we believe they make most sense when the imperative to pray and the abounding grace of God matched with that imperative define their dynamics and implications. For even though the majority of a given people may restrict the significance of their culture to matters of worldly survival or prosperity, their words and actions outrun such a restriction. Each meal that people take has encoded in its symbolism the appeal for daily bread that millions of biblical believers have considered as much spiritual as physical. Each comfort of a child has carried a pledge or petition that all might be well comprehensively, cosmically. The job to which a family looks for security is blessed for providing that, yet no job can secure human beings against pain, so any outflow of gratitude for work goes beyond a particular job to the God who is working always, for human beings' benefit. The coat that a person dons in satisfaction at its good fit and fine material suggests the clothing the spirit must have, if it is to find satisfactions that do not go out of style or become threadbare.

To investigate the character of prayer in the world religions is to enter upon the symbolic interpretation that longing for meaning and security has generated everywhere. Many Africans have dwelt within a forest of symbols, as many biblical peoples have seen allegories and analogies everywhere. The religions of Asia have been much the same, turning over every bit of human experience and imagination in search of divine potential. Judaism and Islam, despite their desire to be stripped of anything compromising the divine oneness, have produced reams of literature about the incarnation of proper piety in daily life.

Prayer is the wellspring and atmosphere of such analogous imaginations. Setting the human spirit in the ocean of the divine Spirit, the immensity of the mystery that tokens the divine presence on all sides, prayer has freed humanity to explore every bit of its experience for ultimate significance. From fingernails to migraines, human beings have picked over the small and the distressing, the grand and the elevating. In all of this they have been searching for God, the ultimate reality that might secure their lives in significance. But, as Pascal saw, they would not have been searching for God had they not already found God. Their very searches have borne the mark of God's inspiration and care. If they have flown to the highest heavens, God could be there. If they have descended to the lowest depths, God could still be there. For if God is God, nothing exists or signifies without implicating God. In God we live and move and have our being. Nothing can separate us from God, because God has chosen to be our beginning, our end, our foundation, our hope. The prayer of the world religions is the richest testimony one can find to the omnipresence of this intuition.

NOTES

1. INTRODUCTION

1. See, for example, John Hick and Paul F. Knitter, eds., *The Myth of Christian Uniqueness: Toward a Pluralistic Theology of Religions* (Maryknoll, NY: Orbis, 1987) and Leonard Swidler, ed., *Toward a Universal Theology of Religion* (Maryknoll, NY: Orbis, 1987).

2. Denise Lardner Carmody and John Tully Carmody, *Peace and Justice in the Scriptures of the World Religions* (New York: Paulist, 1988).

3. Implied here is some criticism of Paul Van Buren's multivolume work *A Theology of the Jewish-Christian Reality* (San Francisco: Harper & Row, 1983 ff.).

2. JUDAISM

1. Ber. 32b, in Arthur A. Cohen, *Everyman's Talmud* (New York: Schocken, 1975), p. 83. The first reference is to the Talmudic tract quoted.

2. Louis Jacobs, *Hasidic Prayer* (London: Routledge & Kegan Paul, 1972), pp. 9–10.

3. Claude Lanzman, *Shoah: An Oral History of the Holocaust* (New York: Pantheon, 1985), p. 14.

4. "Kaddish," *Encyclopedia Judaica*, vol. 10 (Jerusalem: Keter, 1972), p. 660.

5. Cohen, *Everyman's Talmud,* pp. 155–156.

6. Leo Trepp, *Judaism: Development and Life,* 3d ed. (Belmont, CA: Wadsworth, 1982), p. 267.

7. *Gates of Prayer: The New Union Prayerbook* (New York: Central Conference of American Rabbis, 1975), p. 391.

8. Richard Siegel et al., eds., *The Jewish Catalog* (Philadelphia: Jewish Publication Society, 1973), p. 302.

9. See Ninian Smart and Richard D. Hecht, eds., *Sacred Texts of the World: A Universal Anthology* (New York: Crossroad, 1982), pp. 66–67.

10. Trepp, *Judaism: Development and Life,* p. 293.

3. ISLAM

1. See Seyyed Hossein Nasr, ed., *Islamic Spirituality: Foundations* (New York: Crossroad, 1987), pp. 311–409.

2. Cheikh Hamidou Kane, *Ambiguous Adventure* (New York: Collier, 1974), pp. 6–7.

3. Michael Cook, *Muhammad* (New York: Oxford University Press, 1983), pp. 15–16.

4. Kenneth Cragg and Marston Speight, eds., *Islam from Within: Anthology of a Religion* (Belmont, CA: Wadsworth, 1980), p. 80.

5. Saadia Khawar Khan Chishti, "Female Spirituality in Islam," in Nasr, *Islamic Spirituality: Foundations,* p. 205.

6. N. J. Dawood, trans., *The Koran* (Baltimore, MD: Penguin, 1971), p. 15. Unless noted otherwise, quotations from the Qur'an are from this translation.

7. G. D. Newby, "Allah," in Keith Crim, ed., *Abingdon Dictionary of Living Religions* (Nashville, TN: Abingdon, 1981), p. 23.

8. F. M. Denny, "Prayer in Islam," ibid., p. 576.

9. George Appleton, ed., *The Oxford Book of Prayer* (New York: Oxford University Press, 1985), pp. 329–330.

10. Ibid., p. 331.

11. Martin Lings, *What is Sufism?* (Berkeley: University of California Press, 1977), p. 74.

12. See Ninian Smart and Richard D. Hecht, eds., *Sacred Texts of the World: A Universal Anthology* (New York: Crossroad, 1982), pp. 157–158.

13. Joseph Henninger, "Pre-Islamic Bedouin Religion," in Merlin L. Swartz, ed., *Studies on Islam* (New York: Oxford University Press, 1981), p. 10.

4. HINDUISM

1. See R. C. Zaehner, *Hinduism* (New York: Oxford University Press, 1966); Mircea Eliade, *Yoga: Immortality and Freedom* (Princeton, NJ: Princeton University Press/Bollingen, 1970); Heinrich Zimmer, *Philosophies of India* (Princeton, NJ: Princeton University Press/Bollingen, 1969).

2. William Buck, *Mahabharata* (Berkeley: University of California Press, 1973), pp. 6–7.

3. Kees Bolle, trans., *The Bhagavadgita* (Berkeley: University of California Press, 1979), p. 209 (18:51–54).

4. Ibid., pp. 211, 213 (18:63–69).

5. Edward C. Dimock, Jr. and Denise Levertov, trans., *In Praise of Krishna* (Garden City, NY: Doubleday, 1967), p. 29.

6. A. L. Basham, *The Wonder That Was India* (New York: Grove Press, 1959), p. 162.

7. Raimundo Panikkar, *The Vedic Experience* (Berkeley: University of California Press, 1977), pp. 634–635.

8. S. N. Dasgupta, *Hindu Mysticism* (New York: Frederick Ungar, 1977), p. 157.

9. Ibid., pp. 160–161.

10. Basham, *The Wonder That Was India,* pp. 159–160.

11. Gerald D. Berreman, *Hindus of the Himalayas,* 2d ed. (Berkeley: University of California Press, 1962), p. 103.

12. Thomas J. Hopkins, *The Hindu Religious Tradition* (Encino, CA: Dickenson, 1971), pp. 33–34.

5. BUDDHISM

1. William Theodore de Bary, ed., *The Buddhist Tradition in India, China, and Japan* (New York: Vintage Books, 1972), pp. 22–23.

2. Philip Kapleau, *The Three Pillars of Zen* (Boston: Beacon, 1967), pp. 228–229.

3. Melford Spiro, *Buddhism and Society,* 2d ed. (Berkeley: University of California Press, 1982), p. 264.

4. Ibid.

5. Edward Conze, ed., *Buddhist Texts through the Ages* (New York: Harper & Row, 1964), pp. 199–201.

6. In addition to Kapleau's *The Three Pillars of Zen,* see Nyanaponika Thera, *The Heart of Buddhist Meditation* (London: Rider & Co., 1969) and Winston L. King, *Theravada Meditation* (University Park: The Pennsylvania State University Press, 1980).

7. Taitetsu Unno, "Worship and Cultic Life: Buddhist Cultic Life in East Asia," in *The Encyclopedia of Religion,* ed. Mircea Eliade (New York: Macmillan, 1987), vol. 15, pp. 468–469.

8. Ninian Smart and Richard D. Hecht, eds., *Sacred Texts of the World* (New York: Crossroad, 1982), p. 253.

6. NATIVE AMERICAN RELIGIONS

1. See Sam D. Gill, *Native American Religions: An Introduction* (Belmont, CA: Wadsworth, 1982), pp. 46–47.

2. Lawrence E. Sullivan, *Icanchu's Drum: An Orientation to Mean-

ing in South American Religions (New York: Macmillan, 1988), 118–119. See also Michael Harner, *The Way of the Shaman* (New York: Harper & Row, 1980).

3. Florinda Donner, *Shabono* (New York: Delacorte, 1982), pp. 162–163.

4. Joseph Epes Brown, ed., *The Sacred Pipe: Black Elk's Account of the Seven Rites of the Oglala Sioux* (Baltimore: Penguin, 1973), p. 70.

5. Ruth Murray Underhill, *Singing For Power: The Song Magic of the Papago Indians of Southern Arizona* (Berkeley: University of California Press, 1976), pp. 44–46.

6. Joseph Epes Brown, *The Spiritual Legacy of the American Indian* (New York: Crossroad, 1982), p. 91.

7. Sam D. Gill, *Native American Religions: An Introduction* (Belmont: Wadsworth, 1981), pp. 69–71.

8. Emory Sekaquaptewa, "Hopi Indian Ceremonies," in *Seeing with a Native Eye: Essays on Native American Religion,* ed. Walter Holden Capps (New York: Harper & Row, 1976), pp. 38–39.

9. Ake Hultkrantz, *The Religions of the American Indians* (Berkeley: University of California Press, 1979), p. 3.

10. See John Carmody, *Ecology and Religion* (New York: Paulist, 1983); H. Paul Santmire, *The Travail of Nature* (Philadelphia: Fortress, 1985).

11. Carl F. Starkloff, *The People of the Center: American Indian Religion and Christianity* (New York: Seabury/Crossroad, 1974), pp. 132–133.

7. AFRICAN RELIGIONS

1. E. Thomas Lawson, *Religions of Africa* (San Francisco: Harper & Row, 1984), pp. 4–5.

2. Robert Cameron Mitchell, *African Primal Religions* (Niles, IL: Argus, 1977), pp. 20–21.

3. Denise Lardner Carmody and John Carmody, *The Story of World Religions* (Mountain View, CA: Mayfield, 1988), p. 33.

4. Geoffrey Parrinder, *African Traditional Religion,* 3d ed. (New York: Harper & Row, 1976), p. 41.

5. Colin M. Turnbull, *The Forest People* (New York: Simon & Schuster, 1962), p. 92.

6. Colin M. Turnbull, *The Mountain People* (New York: Simon & Schuster, 1972), pp. 185–186.

7. Mircea Eliade, *From Primitives to Zen* (New York: Harper & Row, 1967), p. 269.

8. Denise L. Carmody and John T. Carmody, *Ways to the Center,* 3d ed. (Belmont, CA: Wadsworth, 1989), p. 56.

9. John S. Mbiti, *African Religions and Philosophy* (Garden City, NY: Doubleday/Anchor, 1970), p. 81.

10. Benjamin C. Ray, *African Religions* (Englewood Cliffs, NJ: Prentice-Hall, 1976), pp. 79–80.

11. E. E. Evans-Pritchard, *Nuer Religion* (New York: Oxford University Press, 1977), pp. 145–146.

12. Victor Turner, *The Drums of Affliction* (Ithaca, NY: Cornell University Press, 1981), pp. 114–115.

13. Colin M. Turnbull, *The Human Cycle* (New York: Simon & Schuster, 1983), pp. 226–227.

14. Ali A. Mazrui, *The Africans* (Boston: Little, Brown, 1986), p. 315.

GLOSSARY

Arapaho: Plains Indians of the Algonquin group who lived along the Platte and Arkansas rivers.

Arhat: The saint revered by Theravada Buddhists.

Aryans: Indo-Europeans who invaded India from the Northwest during their second millennium B.C.E.

Bar (Bat) Mitzvah: The Jewish ceremony for coming of age.

Bodhi tree: The pipal tree under which, according to legend, the Buddha gained enlightenment.

Brahma: The first of the three gods in the Hindu trinity.

Chosenness: Being special—sitting in a unique relationship—to God.

Dhammapada: A short ethical treatise that is perhaps the best-loved Theravada scripture.

Dharma: The Teaching that is the second of Buddhism's three "Jewels."

Divination: Attempts to discern the future or discover the cause of misfortune.

Exodus: The Hebrews' deliverance from slavery in Egypt.

The Final Solution: The Nazi plan to solve Europe's troubles by eliminating all Jews.

Four Noble Truths: The core summary of the Buddha's teaching, which states: All life is suffering. The cause of suffering is desire. By removing desire one can remove suffering. The way to remove desire is to follow the noble Eight-fold Path of Buddhist practice.

Gautama: The historical Buddha.

Hajj: The pilgrimage to Mecca.

Mount Horeb: The equivalent or alternative to Mount Sinai, the site of the Mosaic covenant.

Hopi: The westernmost group of Pueblo Indians, located in northeastern Arizona.

Jainism: An ascetical Indian religion founded by the Mahavira a generation before the Buddha.

Kachina Masks: Faces worn by Hopi dancers to make present the spirits shaping Hopi life.

Kosher: Approved, "clean." The Israelites were directed in how to slaughter animals for food and which to avoid for consumption.

Krishna: An avatar (incarnation) of the god Vishnu; the most popular Hindu deity.

Last Day: The end of history, when Allah will render judgment on all peoples' deeds.

Mantra: A sound whose repetition helps focus one's meditation.

Mecca: The capital of Islam, located in Saudi Arabia.

Mende: A Niger-Congo tribe living in Sierra Leone and Liberia.

Navaho: The largest Native American tribe in the U.S., spread throughout New Mexico, Arizona, and Utah.

Nirvana: The state where all conditions fall away, where reality is released from desire.

Nuer: A tribe living along the banks of the Nile in the Southern Sudan.

Passover: The annual commemoration of the Hebrews' exodus from Egypt.

Patanjali: The reputed author of the most authoritative treatise on yoga, *The Yoga Sutra*.

Peyote: An hallucinogenic mushroom used sacramentally by some Native American groups.

Primal world view: The sense of reality shared by adherents of African tribal traditions.

Ramadan: The annual Muslim period for fasting.

Rites of passage: Ceremonies designed to transfer people from one stage of life to another—e.g., from uterine existence to infancy, from childhood to adulthood, from life to death.

Seneca: An Iroquoian Native American tribe who lived in western New York and eastern Ohio.

Shiva: The second most popular Hindu divinity; an erotic ascetic credited with the regular destruction of the world.

Sufi: Mystical Islam; Muslim groups dedicated to religious experience.

Sun Dance: The most famous Lakota ritual, used to rededicate the tribe to its cultural ideals.

Shoshone: A Native American tribe located in California, Nevada, Utah, Idaho, and Wyoming.

Surah: A chapter of the Qur'an.

The Temple: The center of biblical Israel's worship.

Tibetan Book of the Dead: A famous Buddhist manual describing how to shepherd a dying person toward enlightenment and nirvana.

Upanishads: Poetic philosophical or mystical writings found at the end of the Vedas.

Vajrayana: The ritualistic (Tantric) Buddhism dominant in Tibet.

Vishnu: Third member of the Hindu trinity of leading gods responsible for creation.

Yogi: One who strives for release (moksha) by disciplined meditation.

Yoruba: An African tribe living mainly in southwestern Nigeria. The Yoruba were the most urbanized Africans prior to Western colonization.

Zen: The Japanese form of the Buddhist school most focused on meditation.

Zuni: A Pueblo tribe of west central New Mexico.

INDEX

164